My Work My Way

7 Steps to Thriving in the Early Steps of Your Career

Vipin Ramdas

Foreword by **Raymond Aaron**

New York Times Best Selling Author

A very elegantly written book with valuable tips and advice to anyone seeking to excel in the early stages of their career. Vipin does not make any tall claims or give any fancy tips or tricks. The book combines knowledge nuggets from his experience over the last 13 years and provides practical tips and advice which can be applied easily.

Mukund Cairae
President - Middle East North Africa, Turkey & Pakistan,
Zee Network & Ten Sports

Vipin Ramdas has created the perfect roadmap to career success. "My Work My Way "should be mandatory reading for everyone who wants to increase their income, realize their full potential, and achieve greater career success than they ever imagined possible.

Glenn Shepard
Author of the #1 Best Seller
"How to be Employee Your Company Can't Live Without"

There are thousands of books written on how to succeed in your career. What I found different about this book is that it's written by someone who has used the recommendations and tips he gives in his own career to get to where he is today. For any young professional who wonders how to deal with the real issues at hand when starting a career, Vipin provides very pragmatic advice."

Edith Kessler-Charalambous
Senior Director, Client Services
International Services Company

This is one of those clever books I wished I had read many years ago when starting out on my chosen professional path. I found it refreshingly honest and full of good advice given by someone who has clearly experienced the scenarios referred to in the book. Vipin is putting that experience in the hands of those starting out in their career today. They will gain positive insights from his writing. Highly recommended.

Colum G Rafferty
CEO
Aventi Technologies Ltd.

Dedication

To the dynamic, enthusiastic, fun loving and trend setting generation of today. Generation Y!

Acknowledgments

I almost feel like I'm standing up in front of an audience receiving an Oscar. It has been my dream and wish for a long time to write a book, and it's amazing to see the dream come true. I had been procrastinating for so long that I had almost forgotten about it for a while. I am grateful to my mentor Raymond Aaron for presenting me the opportunity, inspiring me and providing guidance in completing this book.

There are a number of people who have helped me realise this dream. First and foremost is my family. I'm truly blessed to have such a wonderful family. I'm madly in love with my wife, even after fifteen years. She is my biggest critic, yet has a strange way of keeping me going and never giving up. I want to thank her for all those days when she pushed me to keep working on the book even when I didn't feel like it. My two sons drive me crazy and there were times during the writing of this book when I wanted to pull my hair out (and sometimes theirs!). Anyone with two young children at home will appreciate how challenging it can be to find any time to do something as serious as writing a book. But they have also been a source of inspiration for me. I hope I make them proud when they read this book one day.

There are two people to whom I owe everything in life for what I am today. It took me some time and the qualification of fatherhood to realise what it means to be a parent. My dad probably does not know this, but he has been my role model. I still remember him giving a talk on leadership and watching the entire auditorium stand up in applause. It was that day that I felt that I wanted to do something similar with my life. My dad is a voracious reader and I've been trying to convince him to write a book himself. I truly believe he has a wealth of knowledge inside him. I hope to convince him one day. My mom is an absolute darling, and like every other mom, for her, her sons can never be wrong. When things are tough, all I have to do is think about all that my mom told me about how I was unique and how I was strong enough to achieve anything in life.

This book would not have been possible had it not been for the wonderful managers I have had in my career. Each one of them has helped me grow and develop as an individual and a professional. Each one has taught me valuable lessons during my journey. It has not been an easy ride, but I never wanted easy. I do feel lucky to have had managers with very different management styles. Apart from helping me grow, it also gave me different perspectives to dealing with similar issues.

This book would not have seen its day had it not been for the support of my wonderful book architect Lori Murphy. Thank you for all the tips, the attention and the hand holding you provided.

Lastly, this book would be incomplete without the help and support from my friends and colleagues. The water cooler discussions, performance review meetings, chats over coffee: all have helped me get an understanding of what the generations in our workplace think about their careers and the other generations.

Thank you everyone for making my dream come true.

Foreword

My Work My Way: 7 Steps To Thriving In The Early Steps Of Your Career is a practical guide for all aspiring young professionals keen to succeed in their careers. It's a no nonsense, straightforward, step-by-step guide on what it takes to find success during the early stages of your career.

What's unique about this book is the fact that it's written for you, the young and dynamic generation (Generation Y) of today. There are plenty of books written on how everyone else (the older generations) should be managing you and get the best out of you. This is one of those few books which are written to help you understand the dynamics of the corporate world and what it takes to be successful amongst your older and more experienced colleagues.

There is no one secret sauce to help you be successful in your career. Rather, it's a combination of skills, techniques and common sense which will get you from where you are to where you want to be. In this book you will find the answers to all the questions which you wanted to ask but didn't know who to ask.

— What is my personal brand and how can I build it?
— How do I make sure I get that promotion I deserve?
— How can I turn my boss into my biggest fan?
— How do I get people to take me seriously when I'm still young and new?
— What are most important skills I will need during the early years of my job?

In this book, Vipin provides practical tips and techniques and busts some of the commonly held myths about career progression. The best part that I like about this book is the simplicity with which Vipin has expressed his ideas. This will go a long way in helping you understand the simple but powerful techniques which you can use to achieve your career goals.

I encourage you to become a student of the principles and techniques described in this book.

Raymond Aaron
New York Times Best Selling Author
Professional Speaker and Success Coach

Table of Contents

Introduction

Don't wish it were easier. Wish you were better.

-Jim Rohn

When I passed out of college, I was lucky enough to have two job offers in my hand and have the luxury of a choice. The world economy was jumping back after a slump and corporations were expanding and looking to recruit fresh talent. As I write this book, it's been six years since the financial crisis started and still one-third of the 93 million unemployed people in the top 20 economies have been looking for work for more than a year. Youth unemployment in the US has reached an alarming 16%, which is double the unemployed rate of adults. The statistics for Europe are worse, with the average youth unemployment at 24% and some countries like Greece and Spain at close to 60% of unemployment amongst youth. The top 20 economic powers of the world are struggling to create enough jobs.

While thinking through the subject for my book, I went through a number of ideas to find the right topic. With my love for talking to the young adults, what I knew was that the topic would have to revolve around the young and dynamic generation (Generation Y) of today. I wanted to share my experiences and knowledge with my younger friends to help them with their careers in these uncertain and difficult times.

What I discovered was that while there have been many books written on helping the baby boomers (people born between 1946 and 1964) and Generation X (born between 1961 and 1980), to help manage the self-confident, tech savvy, enthusiastic and ambitious Generation Y (born after 1982), there were not as many books to help the Gen Y professionals understand what it takes to succeed in their career.

Relations among the generations seem to be at a low point. Gen Y thinks Gen X is a bunch of whiners. Gen X sees Gen Y as arrogant and entitled. And everyone thinks the baby boomers are self-absorbed workaholics. The representatives of Gen Y are criticised regularly for being selfish, thinking only of themselves and prioritising their individual goals. I believe that rather than looking at Gen Y as an individualistic generation, one should view them more as a generation which places greater emphasis on the individual.

Recent research shows that 68 percent of baby boomers feel "younger people" do not have as strong a work ethic as they do and that makes doing their own work harder. 32 percent of Gen X-ers believe the "younger generation" lacks a good work ethic and that this is a problem. And 13 percent of Gen Y-ers say the difference in work ethic across the generations causes friction. They believe they have a good work ethic for which they're not given credit.

We need to move away from these stereotyped definitions used for Generation Y by embracing their views and providing opportunities to freely express their ideas and live their dreams. Most of our education systems around the world are grossly inefficient. Ok, that might be bit of a stretch, but the fact remains that college education was never designed to prepare you for the real world. What college gives you is good quality academic education. Many students graduate without ever having been taught the basic skills you require to succeed in a corporate environment.

As Jim Finklestein puts it in his thought-provoking book *Fuse*, we are in the middle of a very unique phenomenon where corporations have to deal with a cogenerational workplace. What we are seeing today is nothing short of a war of the generations. The Gen X-ers who are now at middle to senior management positions are looking to consolidate and grow their positions. The baby boomers who were supposed to have retired by now are trying to re-enter the job market, either because their life savings and pension plans have dried up or because they are looking for new challenges to keep them busy. This poses a very unique problem to Gen Y-ers. It puts them at head to head competition with a bunch of people who bring with them the wealth of wisdom and the benefit of experience.

Employers are finding it extremely difficult to make choices. Do they recruit someone who has the passion, the drive, the enthusiasm, fresh ideas and the potential to be the star of tomorrow (the Gen Y-ers) or do they fall back on their stars of yesteryear for their leadership experience and emotional stability?

So if you are a Gen Y-er, how do you take on these sumo wrestlers of yesterday? How can you make sure that you have it your way without stepping on the foot of the baby boomers and the Gen X.? How do you make sure that you don't have to work you butt off, yet be successful? How can you ensure that you get the work-life balance you are looking for? Finally, how do you make sure that you are living life to the fullest without hampering your career?

These are questions which this book aims to answer. *My Work, My Way* is a summary of the lessons I have learnt from of my experiences as a Gen X. Having worked with and managed all three generations, I believe I'm uniquely positioned to share this knowledge with my peers and younger friends.

If you belong to the Gen Y and you're holding this book in your hand, it means that you have decided to take charge of your life, take accountability of your career and realise your goals.

This book is filled with snippets of knowledge, experiences and learnings over the past thirteen years of my professional career. During these years I have learnt what it takes to progress in my career, stand out from the crowd and get what I wanted from my career. I have managed people from over fifteen nationalities speaking more than twenty different languages across five different geographies and an equally wide range of cultures.

I sincerely hope that you find this book useful and that you will make use of the information in it to enhance your career and make progress towards your goals. I wish you all the success in your career. Dream big and take bigger actions!

Step 1: Empty Your Cup: Learn by Unlearning

The illiterate of the twenty-first century will not be those who cannot read and write, but those who cannot learn, unlearn and relearn.

−Alvin Toffler

One of my all-time favourite stories is about a conversation between Tokusan, a Buddhist scholar, and Zen Master Ryutan. Tokusan had an extensive background in Buddhist studies and was an expert on the *Nirvana Sutra* (a Buddhist study specialising in Buddha's nature and True Self teachings). He came to study with the master and, after making the customary bows, asked her to teach him Zen. Then he began to talk about his extensive doctrinal background and rambled on and on about the many sutras he had studied.

The Zen Master listened patiently and then began to pour the tea into the scholar's cup until it began to overflow and run all over the floor. The scholar saw what was happening and shouted, "Stop, stop! The cup is full; you can't get any more in." The master stopped pouring and said: "You are like this cup; you are full of ideas and preconceived notions. You come and ask for teaching, but your cup is full; I can't put anything in. Before I can teach you, you'll have to empty your cup."

This story is truer today than ever before. Most of us approach life with preconceived opinions, biased views, baseless assumptions and hidden fears. Unfortunately, a lot of this is based on limited knowledge gained through reading a few books and more recently through the preaching's of various self-proclaimed "experts" on the Internet.

When you take your first step into the corporate world, one of the first things you should practice is to "empty your cup." What this means is you need to start your career with an open mind and look at this day as if you were a child born today. As the famous Zen saying goes, "Knowledge is learning something every day. Wisdom is letting something go every day."

While college does give you high quality education, most of it is purely academic and the reality of the corporate world often comes as a shock to most young professionals. Engineering and Management graduates from some of premier universities around the world get selected from campus by the world's top organizations even before they have graduated. With technological advances, human capital continues to be the most valued resource and corporations are willing to pay the price to get the best of the best.

What all of this has done is create a sense of false entitlement within today's youth. What contributes to this is the upbringing that Gen Y has been through, where you have been encouraged to be self-confident go-getters who were constantly rewarded for things you did.

I don't blame you for wanting more from your careers, for seeking a work-life balance and for being hungry for fast growth. From the time you were born you were encouraged to dream big and work and pursue your passion. And then, when your hopes and aspirations were not met, you ended up constantly changing jobs. What do we do in return? We end up branding you as impatient, disloyal, lazy, rude, demanding, overconfident job hoppers.

While I think this is an unfair stereotype of Gen Y, I also believe that the youth of today need to be empowered and coached on how to excel in your careers and not just survive in the midst of all this paranoia.

The fact remains that today we are living in an era where three generations co-exist in the workplace, and if you plan to work on your passions and achieve your dreams, you need to learn to adapt before you can bring about the change that you want.

There are two ways you could go about your careers. First, you play the victim and complain about your job and how your employer is not being fair and hope to succeed. The second is to take charge of your career by understanding the dynamics of the game and leveraging it to your advantage. In this process you may have to make small sacrifices in the beginning, but the prize at the finishing line will definitely be worth it.

Whether you want to be an ergonomics specialist at Google, a software architect at Microsoft, a content strategist at Facebook, the next sales ninja, finance wizard or any other profession, you are going to have to have to learn the tricks of the trade before you can change them.

1. Prepare For a Brain Dump

You've landed that dream job with one of the leading IT companies in the world. A big pay cheque, a plush office, the latest technology and your first business card! Wow, how cool is that? This is exactly what I felt when I first landed my job. I was eager to put my knowledge to work and shine in front of the world. Thirteen years from that day, I wish someone had explained the simple truths on how colleges were ill equipped to prepare you for corporate life. Slowly but surely I understood that one of the first things I needed to do was to empty my cup and engage in relearning.

Here are my top six tips which will help you prepare for those early days:

a) Use it or lose it.

I love books and what they teach us, but when it comes to corporate life, what's most relevant is the application of that knowledge. It doesn't matter if you got straight A's throughout your academia. If you do not know how to use that knowledge in solving real life problems, you will struggle. When you read a book or learn something new, try to spend time thinking through how and where you can use it in your life. Use it or lose it.

b) The path will not be clear.

Academic life was easy for me. I almost knew where I was going, what was expected of me and how I was going to get there. I knew that if I got a degree and got good grades I would end up getting a job.

Unfortunately, once I got the job, I realised that my honeymoon had ended. No one told me what I was supposed to do. I did not know what my final destination was and the road ahead was often foggy. Understand and accept that it is absolutely ok to feel this way if you do. Don't lose hope. Have patience and engage in continuous action and the path will start becoming clearer.

c) Don't expect much hand holding.

College was so much fun. Friends got together, helped each other out, wrote assignments for each other, copied notes and stood by our backs. On the battlefield of work, you stand alone in making sure you are successful. Don't get me wrong: there are colleagues who will provide you with support and encouragement, but at the end of the day you alone will determine your success.

Don't expect people to spoon feed you with the information you need or give you step by step instructions on how to go about things. Most often than not, things will be vague and you will be expected to get on with things and deliver based on the information available.

d) You don't make friends at work.

When I passed out of college, social media was unheard of. The Internet itself was in its nascent stages. So we spent more time in the physical world with friends from the real world. One mistake I made early on in my career was to trust colleagues to be friends. I learnt the hard way to guard my secrets and confide only in my friends outside of work. So while you should have healthy and nourishing relationships at work, don't mistake them to be your "friends." Of course you should go out and have fun, have beer (or coffee) together and party with your colleagues. But learn to draw the line and know when and where to stop.

e) Looks *do* matter.

When I graduated, we were always taught to dress up well and stay groomed. Over the years, this has diluted and the youth of today seem to have forgotten the importance of dressing up well. Dressing up doesn't mean you have to move around in business suits. It simply means that you package yourself in the way you wish to be branded. People do judge based on appearances, and you don't want to lose out on opportunities because you were not dressed appropriately.

It does not matter what you choose to wear, but make sure you comply with the dress code at work. My smart tip here is to always dress one level higher than you currently are.

f) Texting is cool, but you will have to learn to write.

Social media has changed the way we communicate. These days all you need is less than 120 characters to express how you feel or share an idea. This is great, but your work will require you to write (or type), and its best that you brush up on your writing skills. Majority of corporate communication happens through emails, and writing skills are something which employers put a lot of importance on irrespective of which profession you are in.

2. Dulling The Sense of Entitlement

Webster's defines entitlement as the *belief that one is deserving of or entitled to certain privileges.* One of the biggest concerns and a reason for annoyance for the baby boomers and Generation X is that the young generation carries with them a sense of false entitlement. The perception is that the expectations of Generation Y are not proportionate to the amount of work being put in.

While the opinion is debatable, one of the things that you need to learn early in your career is that you have to first start giving before you can receive.

One of my favourite self-help teachers, Bob Proctor, summarizes this very well and said, "We must willingly give and graciously receive."

It's human nature to be disappointed when things don't turn up as we wished. What do you do when your brilliant idea is turned down by your manager or you are not given the opportunity to present your million-dollar business idea to the board of directors? How do you react when your manager does not approve your request to work from home or does not believe you are ready for the promotion? These are everyday situations which you will experience at your workplace.

The important thing to understand here is that if you are to succeed at your workplace, you will need to manage your priorities and expectations. Here's what you need to keep in mind:

a) **You are entitled only as much as you are perceived to be worth.**

A quick way to start is to realize that nobody owes you anything and that if you want something, you are going to have to work for it. Stop playing the victim and take accountability for your career and take on the role of an innovator, challenger and champion. If you think your organization is not providing you the right opportunities or does not value your contributions, then stand up and do what it takes to make that happen. If it does not work out in the end, don't be afraid to quit and find another organization which will give you the platform and the opportunities.

However, do remember that there is no ideal workplace, and if you end up changing jobs frequently you may not gain much experience or expertise in any area, which will put you at a disadvantage in this world of specialists.

b) **Seek appreciation but stop expecting constant recognition.**

You were given stickers for doing well on your tests and your parents rewarded you for doing well in high school — and now you have graduated college and your parents reward you again. As you enter the corporate world, most of this instant gratification goes out of the window. Don't expect a cheer each time you believe you have done a good job. This mind-set needs to change, as your boss is not going to pat you on the back every time you do something right.

c) **Don't stop yourself from expressing your opinion, but learn to respect the opinions of others.**

This is where a lot of people struggle. The notion that your boss or your company will agree to everything that you have to say will only end up making you feel frustrated. Recognize that while you may have knowledge, passion and enthusiasm, your company has other people who bring experience, expertise and wisdom. You need all these skills to make a successful organization. Don't let this deter you from expressing yourself. Just remember that till you establish some credibility and trust, a lot of your ideas could be shot down.

d)   Define what success means to you.

Most young professionals I meet define career success based on job titles, position, salary or promotions. Spend time thinking through what would really make you feel successful in your career. It could be having the right opportunities, or moving up to management or building a new product or exceeding sales targets. Whatever it is, make sure that you do not judge yourself based on other people's opinions. What other people think of you is none of your business. It's theirs.

e) Stop whining and do something.

Just like your generation, every generation before you have had their share of challenges, issues and obstacles. Every generation starts out in their early 20s broke and working in less than ideal jobs. Luckily, there is sex and alcohol to balance out these financially unrewarding years. Then you get older. You work your way up, you make a little more money, you have sex less and drink less (or more in some cases). There's always a trade-off.

f) Follow your passion, but don't lose sight of reality.

This is one of my personal favourites. I sincerely believe that everyone should follow their passion. We have one life and if we don't live with passion, what are we here for? In the end, it's not how much money you make that ultimately makes you happy. It's whether or not your work fulfils you. The best feeling in the world is getting paid to do what you love.

13

While it's great to keep working on your passion, accept that there will be times when you will have to bite the bullet and make sacrifices today for a better tomorrow. The reality is that initially there will be days when you will need to do work which does not always excite you.

Use this time and invest in yourself and your development and keep working towards your dreams. Accepting reality does not mean you cannot achieve your dreams or follow your passion. It just means that sometimes the time isn't right yet. Believe in yourself and your dreams and be ready to pay the price today.

g)   **Learn to manage up.**

If there is one person apart from you who is important in your career, it is your boss. If you are to get anywhere close to what you deserve, your boss will play a big role in determining how fast you get there. Unfortunately, most colleges do not teach you this skill of how to manage up. Setting expectations, defining clear goals, keeping your boss informed and learning to manage your boss are important aspects of your job. This is so important that I have dedicated an entire chapter in this book on how you can succeed at this.

3. Check That Ego At The Door

The Oxford dictionary defines ego as a "person's sense of self-esteem or self-importance." All of us have egos because all of us consciously or subconsciously have a feeling of confidence and satisfaction about a sense of who we are, what we are and what we have achieved. The degree of confidence may vary, however, the fact remains that we all have an ego. So ego by itself is not a bad thing. What is important is how you deal with your ego and use it to your advantage.

Whenever I think of ego, the story that comes to my mind is that of Abraham Lincoln. Abraham Lincoln was walking on a narrow Washington sidewalk after a rainstorm when he saw his arch political rival, Stephen A. Douglas, walking towards him. There was room on the sidewalk only for one pedestrian and the road was muddy. As the two closed in, Douglas said to Lincoln, "I never step aside for a scoundrel." Lincoln replied, "I always do," and he stepped onto the muddy road.

Ego is reflected awareness or consciousness of your own identity. If you grew up totally alone, with no one around you, you would never develop an ego. An ego is a need, a social need, and an ego is created and developed by those around you. The ego's job is to seek approval, accolades, appreciation and validation. It does this at a high cost, many times forgoing the potential for a great outcome in order to be "right."

This leads many bright and talented professionals to argue or to critique decisions or even to withhold their expertise in order to prove their point. The ego consumes a great deal of energy colluding with others debating the merit of an idea – energy that could be used to add value and to make the idea work.

I have been lucky that I never really had a problem managing my ego, probably due to my upbringing and the friends and social life I had. When you first start your career, there are a few things you can do to have a healthy ego at the workplace.

a) **Swallow your pride and focus on relearning.**

You are fresh out of college and are ready to change the world. You have a degree in computer science backed with an MBA. You join the company you have dreamed of only to realise that you are given mundane tasks of creating presentations, summarising reports and sending follow up emails to clients. You think, *I did not do my master's to come and do this!* When you have this thought, remember that everybody who is somebody started from somewhere when he was a nobody. So swallow your pride and use this time to work on your foundation. Remember, empty your cup!

b) **Get used to feeling like a nobody.**

If this is your first job, or you are new to the industry, it's quite possible that the first few months will be very frustrating and overwhelming. I remember my first six months with my company where I felt like a total failure. I couldn't understand what people were talking about, what all the tech talk was about, nothing! I remember feeling completely miserable. My self-esteem was low and my confidence dwindling. If you feel this way, rest assured that you are on the right track. If you feel strongly about your performance, it means you are passionate about your work, and if you are passionate, trust me, you will make it!

c) **Ask a lot of questions.**

A lot of people are afraid to ask questions. One common reason is because the person feels that the question is stupid. Whether this is your first job, a new role, a new industry or even if you are the CEO of the company, don't stop asking questions. As Allan Pease puts it, "Questions are the answers." When you ask, it shows that you were listening, you want to learn and you are interested in understanding more.

d) Speak up, but don't speak down.

While it's good to ask questions, you also need to know when to shut up and listen. Don't be afraid to express your views, opinions and ideas. But speak only if you really have something valuable to add. There is a famous saying that goes: "Smart people speak because they have something to say. Idiots speak because they want to say something." The trick to finding out if what you want to speak is smart or stupid is to ask yourself this simple question: "Am I asking this because I want to understand or see value in my comment, or is this because I feel I must contribute?"

e) It's ok to be wrong.

It's perfectly fine to be wrong. It's ok if you feel that what you said was obvious to everyone. It's absolutely ok to realise that what you learnt was not how things happen in reality. Don't have the urge to be always right with whatever you say or do. Life is not like that, so why should your career be?

f) Solicit and apply feedback.

Apart from asking questions, make it a point to constantly ask for feedback from your manager, your peers and subordinates. Many people forget the importance of asking for feedback and most books and authors focus on how to give feedback. When asking for feedback, be as specific as possible and ask for things where you did well, areas where you could improve, how you could do things differently, etc. Don't focus only on your job role, but also solicit feedback about the softer skills like interpersonal skills, communication, etc. Once you have received feedback, work on how best to apply it.

A healthy sense of self and the ability to be assertive and confident are definitely skills which are helpful in the world of work. However, letting one's ego take control and crossing the line into arrogance, obnoxiousness and an overactive need to be recognized and "in charge" can be the kiss of death for many a career.

We need egos in the workplace – healthy egos in the workplace. People who are confident, able to stand up for their values, and the organisation's values. We don't need over-inflated egos in the workplace that will slowly and systematically cause a campaign of interpersonal destruction.

Step 2: Prepare Your Launch Pad: Lay Your Foundation

The loftier the building, the stronger its foundation must be. The bigger your goals, the stronger your foundation should be.

-Unknown

A building's foundation is arguably its most important feature. If it is not doing its job, serious negative consequences will arise, and the longer it's not properly doing its job, the more serious the consequences are going to be. The more solid the foundation, the less likely the building is to suffer damage from storms, earthquakes or the settling of the earth with the passage of time. Every part of a building depends upon the foundation for support.

When the architects of the Bhurj Khalifa (standing tall at 818 m/2684 ft) sat down to design the tower, their focus was on its foundation. Before the building could be constructed, two years of groundwork had to be laid, including six months of geotechnical investigation and testing, and a year and a half of excavation and foundation construction.

Over 45,000 m3 (58,900 cu yd) of concrete weighing more than 110,000 tonnes were used to construct the concrete and steel foundation, which features 192 piles buried more than 50 m (164 ft) deep. The construction of the tower is believed to have taken over 22 million man-hours.

This reminds me of a story from the Bible. There were once two men, and each needed to build a house. The first man was foolish, and chose to build on sandy soil where it was easy to access and easy to dig the foundations. In a few short weeks, he was almost finished. The second man was wise, and chose to build his house on a rocky hill, where it was very hard to access and to dig the foundation. He spent many months building his house.

As time passed, a huge storm broke upon the houses of these men. After much rain, a flood swept through the valley and the man's house that was built on the sand was swept away. But the second man who had built on the rocky hill was safe. No matter how hard it rained or how fierce the floods were, his house remained solid and immovable.

Let's ask ourselves the question: What's the foundation of our life? Are we like the foolish man, are our lives built on sand? Are we investing our time and energy on working on our foundation for our careers? We are the architects of our career and life. Have you understood how you need to build your foundation to ensure that you stand the test of time and beat recession and other adverse economic situations? This chapter tells you how you can do that.

If you are to build your career to reach the heights like the Bhurj Khalifa, then you need to start by working on your foundation. What are the secret ingredients that go into building the foundation for your career? Depending on the career you have chosen, there could be many, but irrespective of that, they can all be summarised as below.

1. Walk Before You Run

One of the biggest mistakes I have seen young professionals make is fall into the trap of wanting to add too much value. Conventional wisdom says that you need to show your new organization how smart and talented you are by constantly adding value. Your natural tendency may be to charge ahead, trying to make big contributions and dream up great ideas for new initiatives or changes to impress your colleagues. The problem is that if you do this before you have earned acceptance and before you understand your new organization, you will most likely stick your foot in your mouth and embarrass yourself.

What makes the most positive impression is not showing how much you know, but rather demonstrating the maturity to know how much you don't know. This means eyes and ears open and mouth shut until you learn as much as you can about the company and the people in it.

You need to learn the ropes, to understand the nuances of how things are done, before you can hope to make intelligent suggestions for change or have new ideas accepted. You might have an idea for the best new design of a product the company has ever seen, but you can't sell it until you understand the way the company works.

I remember an interesting conversation which I had with one of my close friends. He was someone who did not believe in the value that consultants delivered compared to the cost of their services. He could not see why someone should be paid thousands of dollars to tell us how we should run our business. For me it was simple. They get paid for the knowledge and experience they possess. More importantly an external consultant can help you see things which you cannot see. This is because you are in middle of the problems and hence cannot see and think outside your box. You can't really determine the price of a service. As they say, beauty lies in the eyes of the beholder, so the price of a product or service lies in the wallet (or the bank account) of the buyer.

The point I'm trying to make here leads me to one of the first things you need to do when you have a new job: master the basics. Mastering the basics simply means learning anything and everything you need to know about the business. This includes the industry, the company, departments, products/services and competitors.

What you need to do is go beyond the standard information available and dig deeper and further into the muck and learn more. Learn it in such a manner as if you owned the business. Get a deep-rooted understanding of the company's vision, goals, financial condition, clients and business outlook. All of this may seem like a lot to do and can be overwhelming. How do you go about doing this? Here are five tips which will keep you ahead of the rest:

a) **Do your homework and study the business.**

Most organisations these days have an online presence and usually have a wealth of information on their company websites. If your company has an Intranet (an internal company website), spend time browsing through information on the site. Read through policy documents, departmental updates, blogs, and news: anything that will increase your awareness about the company.

Ask for materials about the company—such as information about its products and services and/or business strategies—anything that will allow you to gain a little extra knowledge. Jot down key questions you want to get answered and ask your manager to help get them answered for you.

b)   Develop organizational savvy.

Meet people and talk to them about what they do. Don't restrict yourself to meeting people within your department. Reach out to people from different functions and get an understanding of the dynamics of your organisation.

Ask for opportunities to be invited to meetings so that you get to learn how discussions take place in the organisation. This also gives you the opportunity to meet some senior people in the company. I learnt about the movers and shakers of my company through this technique.

Seek out opportunities to work on any projects or internal initiatives. You learn a heck lot more in these groups than in formal training sessions.

c)   Overcome the culture shock.

Every company has its own personality and culture. This, in turn, translates into unique sets of rules and norms – often unspoken and informal.

Organizations want employees who "fit" the culture and enthusiastically embrace it. It is critically important that you take the time to understand the culture and politics of your new workplace. If you don't, you are almost assured of making many dumb and embarrassing mistakes that will hurt your career.

Look for clues about how the company operates. For example, is it an open-door environment, or are formal meetings preferred? How are they conducted? Who needs to be involved? Who do you need to keep in the loop and when? How flexible is your new company when it comes to lunch hours, time off and work arrangements?

The dean of my management institute used to say, "Work through the system and not against it." When it's time for you to start promoting your ideas and bringing about change, you will need to know everything about the company's culture.

d)   Understand the unwritten rules.

The first weeks or months of a job can be difficult because you don't know what you don't know. What are the company's unofficial policies, how do you weave your way through politics that predate you, how does most communication occur in the company? Make sure you understand how things work before you try to change them. There is little you can do to fight the corporate culture. But the more you know and understand about the unwritten rules, the more effective you will be. One rule of thumb: regardless of the corporate culture, always be early to appointments and meetings. It shows respect.

I discovered that doing lunches together with colleagues was a great way to keep myself updated. Be careful whom you go out with initially. There are always a bunch of naysayers who are constant whiners and have nothing relevant to share, and being associated with them will hurt your career.

e)   **Establish your brand.**

Right from the first day you enter your office, you need to be consciously aware of YOU as a brand. Your personal brand is what you will be known for. In other words, it's simply a statement of key benefits which someone will think of or say when they want to describe you.

Even when you are not aware of it, people are constantly judging you and forming opinions about you. You need to view every meeting, every phone call, every email, and every interaction that you have with your colleagues, your manager or your executive as a sales pitch.

There are a number of things you can do to build your brand. Here's a list of my top eleven tips for you:

1. Dress well. No, really well. Appearance makes a man (or a woman).
2. Show a lot of enthusiasm.
3. Demonstrate an eagerness to learn.
4. Never be late for meetings.
5. Don't gossip.
6. Don't make promises you cannot keep. If you make one, do whatever it takes to make it happen.
7. Always deliver things on time, or before time.
8. Focus on quality. Double or triple check your work before you submit it.
9. Build on people's egos by asking them for help as an expert.
10. Offer ideas and suggestions at meetings, but know when to shut up and listen.
11. Stay in the news. Make sure you are seen around in important meetings, discussions and conference calls. The sooner people hear about you, the better.

Branding is such an important aspect that I have a complete chapter dedicated to this subject later on in this book.

2. Go Hard on Soft Skills

While your college degree can help you get your first job, it's the soft skills which you acquire during your career which will play a very active role in determining your growth.

There's a wide variety of information available on the Internet and host of books which have been written on the subject of soft skills. I would like to focus here on the bare essentials which you need to learn and master during the initial years of your career.

a)   Communication skills

No matter which industry you are in, or what type of job you are doing, communication is a critical component in your road to success. Most people I meet tend to have a very narrow view of what it means to have good communication skills. A common misunderstanding is that communications is about how well you can present your ideas and give a convincing speech and convince people to see your point of view. While this is definitely an important aspect, there's much more to this. Below are five communication skills which I believe every young professional should master:

b)   Listening

When we were kids, we were always reminded that we have two ears and one mouth. The thought behind this was to remind us that we should listen more than we talk. Most people only hear what is being said and don't really listen. Hearing is the ear perceiving sound. Hearing simply happens. For instance, you hear while you sleep; you don't have to do anything, it just happens.

Listening, however, is something you consciously choose to do. Listening requires concentration so that your brain finds meaning in words and sentences. Listen to understand, not to reply. Most of the times we are only hearing what the other person is saying and are too eager to respond back and provide our opinion (even when it's not asked for!).

Listening leads to learning. How do you make sure you are listening and not merely hearing? Follow the three simple steps below to gain the most of what is being said:

1. **Remove any distractions**: No emails, no Black-Berry, no instant meeting messages, and no phone calls. Keep away anything that could disturb you.
2. **Stop thinking**: More often than not, we are busy analysing what is being said or busy preparing our responses. Stop. Just listen to what is being said as if it were a radio station broadcasting information.
3. **Repeat what was said**: To make sure you don't lose focus and attention, at regular intervals repeat what was said to make sure you mind stays focussed and knows where it needs to stay.

c)   **Verbal**

Work on your vocabulary. English is a common business language in most countries around the world. Invest your time and money in buying books which will improve your vocabulary. Set goals to learn at least one new word every day. The worst thing that can happen is that you are looking for words in the middle of a conversation or a presentation. One of the best ways I have learnt to improve my vocabulary and understanding of the English language is to learn the etymological meaning of words.

The most powerful book I have come across on this is *Word Power Made Easy* by Norman Lewis. Improve your command over the English language. Now, just like me, English may not be your first language. That really does not have to stop you from improving your command over the language. If you are in a country where English is not the business language, master that language. The bottom line in all of this is that you need to have the power of words at your fingertips to be able to communicate effectively.

Another important aspect of verbal communication is the tone and pace of your voice. In his book *Silent Messages*, Professor Albert Mehrabian concludes that 38 percent of communication is based on the tone of your voice. When I was in college, I used to read aloud the editorial section of the daily newspaper to listen to how I spoke. Even today I make it a point to read aloud the editorial sections of leading newspapers across the globe at least once a week. This helps with improving my voice quality, hearing how others hear me, and paying attention to the finer aspects of my voice like tone, pitch, pace and modulation.

d)   Writing

Learn to write well. Or should I say, learn to type well! People will judge you based on your ability to express yourself clearly in your emails, reports, and presentations. Here again, people tend to misunderstand what it means to write well. You don't have to be dramatic in your writing or use complex words to convey your message. Use simple sentences but make sure there are no spelling mistakes and grammatical errors. Technology has made it almost impossible for you to get this wrong these days. Use the inbuilt spell checker and grammar check available in most productivity tools to make sure your writing conveys professionalism and clarity.

Learn to present your ideas using the commonly used tools. Take a course in Microsoft Office to learn some cool tips and tricks. There are thousands of free courses online on how to use Word, Excel and PowerPoint.

e)   **Body language**

In *Silent Messages*, Albert Mehrabian concludes that 55 percent of communication actually takes place through body language. People intuitively and instantaneously develop a perception in the first moments they see you, and body language builds, confirms, or dispels those impressions.

Charlie Chaplin and many other silent movie actors were the pioneers of non-verbal communication skills; they were the only means of communication available on the screen. Each actor was classed as good or bad by the extent to which he could use gestures and other body signals to communicate effectively.

Studying body language and implementing its principles is a subject in its own right and there are hundreds of books written on this subject. One of my favourite authors and an authority on this subject is Allan Pease. I would highly recommend that you read his book *The Definitive Book of Body Language* if you are serious about mastering this skill. You may also want to download a copy of the free eBooks I'm giving away on my website http://www.myworkmywaybook.com which will help you get started on the art of body language.

Below are my Top Five must do's of using body language:

1.   Take care of personal appearance

I come from the old school of thought and firmly believe that your personal appearance creates the first impression about you. While Steve Jobs' turtleneck made him a fashion icon; he could only pull it off because he was Steve Jobs.

So unless you are a Steve Jobs, I would highly recommend that you pay attention to how you dress. While dressing well will not clinch the deal for you, it will definitely help create the right first impressions.

2.   Develop a good handshake.

For those cultures that value the handshake, much meaning is transferred by the manner in which you offer your hand and the method with which you shake the other person's hand. Some people make instant judgments about your character as a result of your handshake, so it pays to make sure it's conveying what you want it to. Try and be the first to extend your hand. This conveys a positive and friendly emotion to the other person. It also conveys a message that you are willing to take the lead. When you extend your arm, choose to have your palm facing sideways. Never should your palm be facing upwards.

You may sometimes extend your palm facing downwards, which demonstrates a position of authority, and you usually do this with your subordinates and sometimes with your peers. Your handshake should be firm, but don't try and crush the other person's hand.

3. Maintain eye contact.

Always, and I mean *always*, maintain eye contact with the audience. It doesn't matter if you are talking to one person or addressing a group of people. Never look away from your audience. Looking down or away from your audience breaks the sense of trust and also gives people an opportunity to engage in idle thinking.

4. Have a pleasant smile.

This one is straightforward. Always have a smile on your face. Learn to smile with your eyes. Smiling communicates a positive message to your audience and shows you as self-confident, composed and someone who is in charge of the situation.

5. Maintain a good posture.

Last but not least: walk around as if you owned the company. Maintain a good solid posture when talking to people, and especially when addressing a group. When you walk, show a sense of urgency; don't drag your feet as if you were just out of the hospital bed.

f)   Interpersonal skills

There's a famous quote you will find often mentioned in corporate circles. "It's business, not personal." I don't agree with this because I strongly believe that everything is personal. We are human beings who have feelings and emotions. So what happens in the workplace is definitely personal. What you need to develop is the art of managing this so that you can use it to your advantage.

1.   Manners and etiquette

As children, we were taught to mind our manners. Somewhere down the line, we tend to forget about this. A survey found that 86 percent of employers consider business etiquette and protocol intelligence among their most important hiring criteria, and any employee who possesses the skills could be an asset to any organization.

When your boss calls and you're in the middle of a meeting with a colleague, you answer it. It must be important – after all, it's your boss! No, you don't! If you are in a meeting with your team member and you constantly check your emails or are busy replying to emails and do not pay attention to what is being said, your team member will draw negative conclusions about your manners.

It's easy to get caught up in your own tasks and projects. People's focus gets so narrow that they forget to consider the impact that their words or actions will have on other people.

In an attempt to be efficient and productive, we take liberties with our manners at work. Manners and etiquette are more important at work than in our social lives. Depending on which country you are in, the norms for manners and etiquette may differ. If you are in a foreign country, invest time in understanding local mannerisms and etiquette.

2. Sociability

Man is a social animal and the workplace is our jungle. If the jungle needs to maintain its harmony, then it's essential that you develop social skills. Sociability traits are comprised of a set of interpersonal skills and personal characteristics that help you get along with others. Possessing sociability traits means that you are friendly, outgoing, courteous, tactful and diplomatic. You seek pleasure and fulfilment from your relationships.

Being sociable does not mean that you have to spend every evening at the downtown bar drinking beers (or coffee if you prefer that) with your colleagues or accepting every lunch invitation you receive. It simply means that you choose to have a social life with your office colleagues both inside and outside of work. In other words, it's ok to engage in small talk sometimes, talk to people about their personal lives (if the local culture allows this), share a meal with your colleagues and go out for the occasional drinks. Just bear in mind not to overdo it as you may be seen as someone who is very casual and people may not take you seriously at work because of it.

3. Followership

Followership can be defined as the willingness to cooperate in working towards the accomplishment of the group mission, to demonstrate a high degree of teamwork and to build cohesion among the group. One challenge with young professionals is their ability to be a follower. I firmly believe that a great leader should begin by being a great follower. Someone who does not know how to follow will not be a successful leader. During the initial stage of your career, it's essential that you learn the skills of becoming a good follower. Here are some of my tips:

I. Support your boss, don't undermine.

It is very easy to put the blame of an unpopular policy or decision on your boss. Very often I hear people say things like, "I don't agree with this, but we have to do it because this is what the boss wants us to do."

While this may win you some affection with your peers or your subordinates, this demonstrates disloyalty to your manager and to the organisation. It's ok to disagree with your boss. However, if a colleague asks you whether or not you agree with a particular decision, your response should be that it is an irrelevant question; the decision has been taken, and we will now carry out the task. That's what good team players are expected to do.

II. Fight with your boss, but privately.

Followership does not mean you have to blindly follow everything your boss tells you. Don't be a "yes-man." You have an intellect of your own and if you have strong reservations about an issue under discussion, you have an obligation to express them. There is a tendency to tell the boss what you think he or she wants to hear. Resist the temptation. Fight for your people and your organization; don't roll over on principles or on any issue that you believe will be detrimental to accomplishment of the unit's mission.

As a rule of thumb, you should be willing to revisit an issue three times: don't give up after the first discussion or even the second if you are in earnest.

III. Make the decision and then run it by your boss.

This is something I learnt from my last manager. We all believe we are smart enough and mature enough to get the job done without someone hovering around and providing detailed guidance. There is another side to that coin, however. It reminds me of how the soldiers at war are always waiting on their commander to give them orders. While this may make sense on the battlefield, the workplace is a different zone.

While you may believe that your manager is a micro manager, the fact is that very few people actually like to be bombarded with problems that require them to devise solutions. Even the most "hands-on" supervisors would generally prefer that someone present them with a workable plan and ask for their ratification. So the next time you are confronted with an issue, make a decision and then run it by your boss before executing it. As you gain trust with your boss, you can take decisions and inform your boss without having to seek ratification.

IV.   Take ownership and accept responsibility.

This is probably the most important quality of a good follower. While this is a quality you would expect in a leader, I believe it's equally important to possess this as a follower.

Seek out opportunities where you can take responsibility for an outcome and then take full ownership of the results. Accept tasks and assignments even if they seem outside your job description. These will help you develop beyond your job role. Before you become a leader, act like one.

V.   Teamwork

You've probably heard this before a zillion times. Become a team player and learn to work with your colleagues and peers in an amicable manner. At the end of the day, all of us are here to achieve a common goal and fulfil a common vision for the organisation we work for. History stands testament that none has done it alone.

VI.   Be likeable

This is a slightly controversial one. I have heard people having differing opinions about this. My view is that if you are not likeable, people will not want to work with you. Now, being likeable does not mean that you have to say "yes" to everyone's demands and put other people's priorities above yours. It simply means that you need to be seen as someone approachable, having a good sense of humour, showing respect, being genuinely concerned about people, demonstrate honesty, and show empathy. The essence here is to be able to give and earn respect without losing the human touch.

4.   Build Bridges, Invest in Relationships

One of the things that I learnt early in my career was the importance of meeting people and building relationships. The relationships you build will lay the foundation of where and how your career will develop in the years to come. Building relationships does not mean making friends at work, and to be honest, I don't agree you can or should have too many friends at work. One of the reasons is that it can sometimes become challenging dealing professionally with a friend. What's worse is that you could end up being your friend's manager someday, and it becomes extremely difficult to manage the relationship of a boss and a subordinate.

What I mean by building relationships is to build strong professional relationships with people in your organisation and the industry. Get out there and go and meet people. The trick here is that you really need to build a network. There is an age-old saying which states, "Your network is your net worth." I look at this slightly differently. While it's good to meet people and know all the important people, eventually your success will be determined not so much by whom you know, but more by who knows you.

I have learnt to build relationships with my peers and seniors in other departments and when an opportunity came up, these relationships helped me in seeking out these opportunities. Besides putting you on the radar, it also gives your ego a personal boost when someone contacts you directly and asks if you would be interested in taking up the opportunity.

Having a good network and ensuring visibility does not in any way undermine that you have to be really good at what you do. A network will only guarantee that you are privy to the maximum opportunities within the organisation. If you don't have the right skills and experience for the job, the best network cannot help you. Where the network gives you an advantage is a slight edge when your competition is very close. This is one of the reasons why sometimes people feel that even though they were more qualified and fit for the role, they did not get the offer.

While having a network is important, what is critical is that you have the right kind of people in your network. Your network needs to consist of decision-makers or decision influencers. Don't just go with the title of the person; rather look at people who are constantly present in meetings, people whose views and opinions are accepted. These are the people who are the influencers and very often every senior manager will have such a trusted lieutenant whom he or she turns to for advice.

Building a network takes time. This is why you need to start doing this right from the day you arrive on the first day in your new job. Seek out opportunities to meet people and be attentive during meetings to take notice of the influencers.

Do your research by talking to people to find out who are the stars in the organisation. These are people who have achieved success within the organisation and have progressed their way to the top. Pay special attention to this lot and gain an understanding of how they have risen up. What skills do they have that others don't, what's different about the ways they go about doing their day to day business, how they communicate, how they carry and present themselves.

I often get asked how we can understand someone else. Obviously, no one has the time or the inclination to sit down and give you an interview.

So:

1.   **Observe them in meetings.**

Be very attentive in meetings and observe these people during meetings. High performers are usually the people who are leading the meetings and driving them.

By leading, I do not mean the chairperson of the meeting or the one facilitating the meeting. I'm talking about participants whose views and opinions are discussed and agreed upon: people who steer the communication towards their way of thinking. Take notes on how they went about doing this and how they conduct themselves during the meeting.

2.   Analyse their communication style.

Top performers have developed excellent communication skills. When they communicate, people take notice and know that they mean business. If possible, try and attend presentations done by these people, and read and analyse their writing style.

3.   Ask other people.

This is not always easy but can be useful, especially if you have built a relationship with someone who has worked with the performer. Ask these people about what they think of the leader's management style, skills and qualities. Very often they will reveal small secrets which prove invaluable.

4.   Seek advice.

Where appropriate, seek advice from these people by presenting them with some challenges and difficult situations. Most people will be happy to offer you advice on how they would deal with the situation, and this will give you an idea on their thought processes and problem solving techniques.

5.   Ask to be mentored.

If your organisation has a formal mentoring programme, ask to be mentored by one of these stars. If your company does not have a programme, you can still go ahead and ask these people directly.

Most will accept your request and the only caveat will be the actual amount of time they will be able to give you. Whatever time you get with them, it will be quality one on one time with the stars. That's a really big deal!

If you would like a mentor but can't find the right one at work or prefer to have one outside of work, visit my website http://www.myworkmywaybook.com and register to get a discount for one on one coaching from me.

Step 3: Keep Your Eye on the Horizon: Focus

Shoot for the moon. Even if you miss, you'll land among the stars.

-Les Brown

A man came across three masons who were working at chipping chunks of granite from large blocks. The first seemed unhappy at his job, chipping away and frequently looking at his watch. When the man asked what it was that he was doing, the first mason responded, rather curtly, "I'm hammering this stupid rock, and I can't wait 'till five when I can go home."

A second mason, seemingly more interested in his work, was hammering diligently, and when asked what it was that he was doing, answered, "Well, I'm moulding this block of rock so that it can be used with others to construct a wall. It's not bad work, but I'll sure be glad when it's done."

A third mason was hammering at his block fervently, taking time to stand back and admire his work. He chipped off small pieces until he was satisfied that it was the best he could do. When he was questioned about his work he stopped, gazed skyward and proudly proclaimed, "I am building a cathedral!" Three men, all doing the same job, three different attitudes.

This is one of my favourite stories when it comes to how perspectives and attitude can change the way you look at your work. With startling clarity, this story illustrates that purpose has the power to transform not only our attitude about the work that we do, but the quality of our work as well. And if purpose can help one transcend even a physically laborious task as that undertaken by the three masons in our story, then imagine the impact that clarity of purpose can have on our work.

Most people struggle to really see the big picture and recognize the true purpose of their role. It's very important that you try and get an understanding of what kind of work you like to do. This does not necessarily have to be your passion, but it has to be something which you get excited about and enjoy doing.

What I mean by this is a high level understanding of the type of job you like to do. For example, I realised in the fifth year of my professional career that I love writing and interacting with people and simplifying things for people to understand.

I like to look at my career as a continuous relay where we move from one point to another and then another and achieve our goals along the way. You need to stay focussed on your immediate goals and learn and grow along the way.

1.   Don't Shoot a Moving Target

A lot has been spoken and written about setting goals in life. Personal goals, health goals, financial goals, the list goes on. Goal setting is a very important part of your career because if you don't know where you are going, how are you going to figure out how you are going to get there?

Your manager will probably set goals for you each year which will be aligned with your department's goals and eventually to the overall organisations goals. However, these are not *your* goals. These are the company's goals assigned to you to deliver. If you are lucky, you may have some personal developmental goals included along with these but these again are geared to help you support the corporate goals. While there is nothing wrong with this approach, it does not necessarily ensure your growth in the areas which will have the maximum impact.

I set my own career goals as a result of conversations I have had with my manager, events which may have triggered me to identify areas where I need to develop. These could be simple things like learning how to use styles in Microsoft Word to something slightly longer term like improving my relationship with my manager.

This book is not intended to show you how to set your goals. There are plenty of theories and techniques you can Google. A very popular and my personal favourite is the SMART technique. It stands for Specific, Measurable, Achievable, Relevant and Time Bound. It's probably the technique used my majority of the organisations as it's a no nonsense approach to defining what you want (Specific), when you want it by (Time Bound), why you want it (Relevant), how will you know when you have got it (Measurable) and ensuring you can actually get it (Achievable).

Follow these simple ground rules when setting your goals:

a) Look beyond money.

I want money, I know you want it, and everyone wants money. Well, maybe not everyone. While setting your career goals, however, learn to look beyond money. If your sole goal in career is to earn more money, then I'm afraid you may not get too far.

If you are like most people, I'm sure money is not the only motivator for you. I can tell you from experience that when you focus your energies on delivering results for you and the company, the money will come.

I have received salary increments, promotions and bonuses from my company when I least expected them. I used to wonder why this kept happening until I realised that money was not really a big motivator for me, which helped me focus on doing a good job. Now, that does not mean money cannot be a motivator for you, but while setting your goals try and keep it out of your career goals. Money should of course be a part of your financial goals.

b) Focus on big impact in small packages.

Set small goals to start with. This will help you focus on what's important to you. While you should have a long-term view on where you would like to be in ten to fifteen years, what's equally important is to have a good grip on your short-term goals you would like to achieve in one to two years. You may not have all the answers on how you are going to reach your long-term goal, but trust me that you will figure it out as you go along the way.

Your career is like a skyscraper overlooking the sea, and as you climb each floor you start seeing further into the horizon. You have to climb each floor to keep moving towards the top. There are no shortcuts. I guess this is the reason it's called the corporate ladder. So set short-term goals which will eventually help you reach the top. This is extremely important, as you will need the constant motivation of achievement at regular intervals to keep you going.

c) **Personal innovation.**

Transformation rarely happens all at once, instantly. The key is to live in feeling and in this way encounter a continuous, daily stream of revelatory clues as to who and what you truly are, and what you can become. Get into the practice of personal innovation. Very often innovation is associated with a dramatic change or something that is revolutionary. The Oxford dictionary defines innovation as "making changes in something established, especially by introducing new methods, ideas, or products."

So personal innovation is to try and do something new and different to what you have been doing. When setting goals, ensure that you are stretching yourself out of your comfort zone and listing goals which will challenge you. This is the zone where growth happens. You don't have to do great things to be successful. Do the small things every day in a great way and success will follow.

d) Personal growth before personal achievement.

This one's a tricky one. I do not intend to undermine the importance of achievement. Rather, my point here is that the focus should be on ensuring that you go through a process of personal growth every day. You may sometimes not achieve your goals. What's key is that you learn and grow in the process.

This reminds me of a quote from one of my favourite authors, James Allen, in his timeless classic *As a Man Thinketh*. "Even if you fail again and again to accomplish your goals as you must until weakness is overcome; the strength of character gained will form a new starting point for future triumph."

Many believe that we are growing every day due to the activities we undertake every day. Activities like reading newspapers, magazines, talking to people are helping us grow. While this is true, this is *passive* growth rather than *active* growth. You do not have a goal plan for your growth. You do not know what you want to become or be; you just are. This kind of growth does not help us build strength of character. On the contrary, it actually harms us.

Someone once said something interesting about newspapers these days: "If you don't read newspapers you are uninformed. If you read them you are misinformed." So make a conscious decision as to what books you read, what you listen to, what you watch and what relationships you build. Ask yourself this question from time to time: "How did the event or episode help me in my growth?"

2. Bite Off More Than You Can Chew.

In Chapter 2, I asked you to walk before you can run. This works fine when you are still new to the organisation and are trying to figure out things and establish a base.

Once you have established your base, you need to move fast to make sure you stay ahead of the pack.

Now is not the time to relax, rather it's the time to take things head on and go for the home run. Now this doesn't mean that you go around accepting every project that comes your way and saying yes to every assignment out there. You still need to prioritise and decide which of the things are going to help you to take you towards your goals.

You need to look out for opportunities out there which will help you grow, volunteer for initiatives and projects which will enhance your skills, network with as many people as you can, and finally learn as much as you can. Now, to some this may sound like a recipe for stress, burnout and disaster. The reason for this is that most people do not know how to stretch themselves without causing burnout. It is a well-known fact that development and growth happens when we get out of our comfort zone and stretch ourselves.

This could be physical, mental, social or spiritual. For example, all body builders know that if you want muscle growth you need to stretch your muscles beyond the point of resistance. The body quickly starts adapting to the new levels of stress. Although the actual muscle growth happens later on, the stretching gives fuel to the body for that growth. Similarly, exercising your brain builds up mental

endurance and focus. Here are my top tips on how to successfully bite more than you can chew without getting
stressed and burnt out:

a) Work off an urgent/important matrix.

This is one of the simplest but most powerful tools
that everyone should use. It's a simple matrix
which has four quadrants, and you classify the
things you want to do into the 4 quadrants.

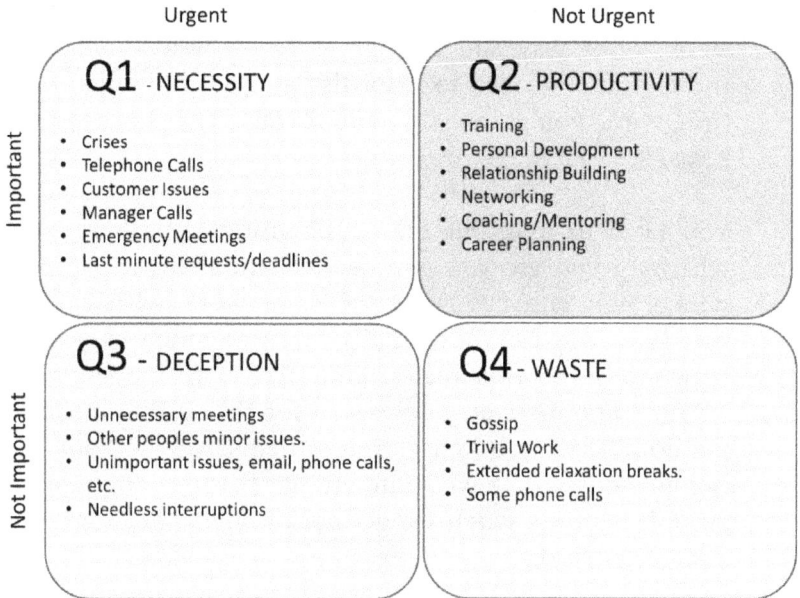

	Urgent	Not Urgent
Important	**Q1** - NECESSITY • Crises • Telephone Calls • Customer Issues • Manager Calls • Emergency Meetings • Last minute requests/deadlines	**Q2** - PRODUCTIVITY • Training • Personal Development • Relationship Building • Networking • Coaching/Mentoring • Career Planning
Not Important	**Q3** - DECEPTION • Unnecessary meetings • Other peoples minor issues. • Unimportant issues, email, phone calls, etc. • Needless interruptions	**Q4** - WASTE • Gossip • Trivial Work • Extended relaxation breaks. • Some phone calls

- Important activities have an outcome that leads
  to the achievement of your goals, whether these
  are professional or personal.
- Urgent activities demand immediate attention,
  and are often associated with the achievement
  of someone else's goals

Urgent activities are often the ones we concentrate on; they demand attention because the consequences of not dealing with them are immediate.

The Urgent/Important Matrix is a powerful way of thinking about priorities. Using it helps you overcome the natural tendency to focus on urgent activities, so that you can keep clear enough time to focus on what's really important.

This is the way you move from "fire fighting" into a position where you feel in control of the circumstances and can grow yourself and your career. Review and update this matrix at the beginning and end of each day/week to stay focussed.

b) Act on the important. Don't react to the urgent.

If I gave you a bowl with a collection of big rocks, small pebbles and some sand and asked you to fit all of these into the bowl, how do you think you would go about doing it? If you are like most of us (smart), then you would first place the big rocks, then put in the small pebbles and lastly try and fit in the sand. Our lives and careers are very similar to this example.

You need to first fit in the important things in your life, followed by the urgent things. Plan your week and day in such a manner so that you have first booked time for activities in the Important/Not Urgent quadrant. Never book your day back to back with meetings. Always keep a contingency of at least one hour for the urgent work which may come your way.

c) Spend an extra hour working.

Before you start thinking about giving up your work-life balance, I want to tell you that this is not about invading your personal time. Notice that I mention spending an extra hour working and not spending an extra hour *at* work. There's a big difference. It is estimated that people routinely waste 15 to 30 minutes at both ends of the workday mentally and physically preparing for the work and home transition. Your productive workday actually starts when you begin working and ends when you start getting ready to go home. Learn to recognize this and leverage this time. For example, use the 15 minutes at the end of the day to plan what you have to complete the next day. This simple action will make sure that you are immediately productive every day when you start your work and don't juggle around wondering what you have to do during the day and worst be driven by other people's demands.

It's amazing how much time is lost in non-productive activities in a day. Some of these things you might not even realize you do because they are now habit. Make an honest list of personal things that you do during your workday. Think about things like futile browsing, idle chit chat, that extra 10 minutes after the coffee break, those extended smoking breaks, unnecessary meetings, etc. Eliminate what you can, and you will be surprised at the amount of free time you find.

d) Ask for help. Don't try and do it alone.

One of the biggest mistakes I made during the early parts of my career was to try and do everything myself. While I was delivering results and achieved a lot, I was stressing myself in the process. When you take on a task or a project, ask for help from people who may have done it before or have some level of expertise. While it's good to learn from your own mistakes, it's better to make new mistakes rather than the same ones which someone else made. If you get stuck with something, ask people around you. You will be surprised how willing people are to help. Make sure that you give them credit where due for helping you in any part of your project or task.

e) Have set times to respond to emails.

Constantly checking incoming email interrupts your workflow, resulting in a productivity slump. Minimize or even better close your email application and schedule times for opening it to check messages. Open, file or delete and print messages at those set times. Use the *two-minute rule* when reviewing your email.

Go through the email and take one of the actions below:

1. Take action on the email if it will take no more than two minutes.
2. Delegate it if you think it's something someone else should do.

3. If you must do it and it will take more than two minutes, book time off to act on it.

The important thing is to act on the email immediately. Most of us (including myself in the past) are guilty of reading the same email at least three times before we decide what to do with it. What a waste of time!

f) Multi-tasking is for computers.

When it comes to work, focus on doing one thing at a time and doing it well, to avoid a fractured thinking pattern, which is neither time-efficient nor productive. Multi-tasking is only for robot-type tasks.

g) Respect your personal life.

Last, but most important, is to respect your personal life. Discipline yourself to leave at a fixed time with a small flexibility of 15 to 30 minutes. Enjoy your time off on weekends and wherever possible completely disconnect from your work. Your body and mind need to relax and rejuvenate to be prepared for another week of productive work.

In the past eleven years of my career, I have never once worked on a weekend. Now, I know some of your work may require you to work on weekends. All I'm saying is that; make sure you are only working when there is a "need", not because someone "wants" you to work. I can't decide this for you and you are the best judge of whether your work can wait till the next working day. I live my life based on a simple philosophy. When you are in your deathbed, you will always wish you spent more time with your loved ones, and not that you spent more time at work.

While a lot of this may sound like time management techniques, the fact is that for you to bite off more than you can chew, you need to either have a bigger mouth or chew faster. Chewing faster (doing things fast) can often be unproductive. However, if you can have a bigger mouth (i.e. create more time), then you stand a good chance of being able to bite off more and more.

Many people think if they could just do more things faster, they'd be more productive. Their brains are hijacked by incoming demands; they lose the ability to discern between important and unimportant priorities. Biting off more than you can chew requires you to be disciplined and productive. If you follow the tips I have suggested, I can guarantee that you will start seeing a positive difference within days. You may also be interested in downloading a free copy of an eBook on Time Management by visiting my website www.myworkmywaybook.com.

3. Going That Extra Mile.

Every job description has a minimum set of requirements to perform the job successfully, but no description ever defines the maximum; what it takes to go above and beyond a job's minimum requirements is up to the individual. Going the extra mile has helped me establish a fulfilling and enjoyable career. Going the extra mile does not necessarily mean to work long hours or being a victim of taking on too much work. On the contrary, it is the art of doing the best you can with what you have and where you can. While each individual's "extra mile" is different, here are five ways you can give more to your job or the profession to get the most out of both:

a) **Think beyond job descriptions.**

Your job description exists only for legal purposes. If you are one of those who constantly have issues about the work given to you on the premise that it's not within your job description, I'm afraid you may not go very far in your career. We are living in an era where it has become increasingly difficult to confine our jobs into the box of a job description. Inevitably all job descriptions these days have a "catch all" clause which indicates that the job description includes any other tasks commensurate with the job title. I'm not suggesting that you become your manager's personal assistant (unless of course you are already one). You have to maintain your dignity and posture and be open to assignments which you believe will leverage your skills or help you enhance them.

b) **Look beyond the transaction. Focus on the relationship.**

Always remember to have the person in mind when working on anything. At the end of the day, an organisation is made up of people who are expected to come together to deliver the same goal.

If you focus beyond the immediate task in hand and look at ways to improve your relationships, you will start getting better results. For example, if you know that you can offer more than what is being asked of you and it can be beneficial to your manager, go ahead and do it. If you have a special skill in using a tool and see a colleague struggling, offer to help him even if it's not your responsibility to train them. Learn to bite the bullet sometimes if you think it will help improve the relationship. Biting the bullet is to give in to someone or a point of view. Doing so at the right time will help nurture and build relationships for the longer term.

c) **Always deliver the best you can.**

I always ask myself a question when asked to deliver something. If this was for someone I loved, how would I do it? Now, I know this may sound far-fetched, especially if the person is your manager or someone who you do not particularly like. The point however is that you should strive to excel in anything that you do. This reminds me of a famous anecdote.

A man once visited a temple under construction where he saw a sculptor making an idol of God. Suddenly, he noticed a similar idol lying nearby. Surprised, he asked the sculptor, "Do you need two statues of the same idol?" "No," said the sculptor without looking up, "We need only one, but the first one got damaged at the last stage." The gentleman examined the idol and found no apparent damage. "Where is the damage?" he asked. "There is a scratch on the nose of the idol," said the sculptor, still busy with his work. "Where are you going to install the idol?" The sculptor replied that it would be installed on a pillar twenty feet high. "If the idol is that far, who is going to know that there is a scratch on the nose?" the gentleman asked. The sculptor stopped his work, looked up at the gentleman, smiled, and said, "I will know it." Set high standards for yourself and people will respect you for your work.

d) Put yourself in the other person's shoes.

You have heard this before and will hear it from others as well. Always be thinking like a customer when you are delivering a service. The service could be anything like sending an email, preparing a presentation, submitting a report or anything else. The customer could be anyone including your boss, peer or even your team member. If you were the customer, what would you expect from the other person? Now focus on delivering this to your customer.

e) Under promise and over deliver.

Under promise and over deliver. How many times have you heard that phrase? Chances are if you've been in business longer than a week, you've heard it at least once if not a dozen times. This does not mean that you constantly underplay what you can do. On the contrary, it means being prudent when you make commitments and factor in contingency time or resources. I know this is easier said than done, however, it is possible. One of the things you will need to do is to be able to make a fairly accurate estimate of what you can do and within what time frames.

When you under promise and over deliver, you have to have a bottom line – in your case, it is simply that you will never deliver late or deliver short. That's it. If you have to sweat blood and work all night then so be it. You will deliver when you said you would – or earlier if you can – without exception. It is better to negotiate a longer delivery time in the first place than to have to let someone down. A lot of people are so keen to be liked, or approved of, or praised that they will agree to the first delivery time offered to them – "Oh yes, I can do that," and then they fail.

Remember that going the extra mile isn't done for self-ish reasons, even though you do end up with much more. You may know in the back of your mind that going the extra mile is beneficial to you, but you really do it because it's the right thing to do. It feels good.

Step 4: Work on Me Inc.: If You Are Not a Brand, You Are a Commodity

Be yourself, everyone else is taken.

– Oscar Wilde

A young but earnest student approached his master and asked: "If I work very hard and diligently, how long will it take for me to find enlightenment in my life?" The master thought about this, and then replied, "Ten years." The student then said, "But what if I work very, very hard and really apply myself to learn fast – how long then?" The master replied, "Well, twenty years." "But, if I really, really work at it. How long then?" asked the student. "Thirty years," replied the master. "But I do not understand," said the disappointed student. Each time that I say I will work harder, you say it will take me longer. Why do you say that?" The master replied, "When you have one eye on the goal, you only have one eye on the path."

We need to keep both eyes on the path, demonstrating that, unlike any other experience in our lives, enlightenment is truly about the journey and not the destination. We need to have patience in order to stay focused on what we want to do.

There is no short cut. We don't get the chicken by smashing the eggs; they need to be hatched.

This story reminds me of the importance of working on ourselves if we are to excel in our lives. Most people work very hard, but they work hard at their jobs and not on themselves. By now you probably realise that if there's one person who will determine if you will be successful in your career, it's YOU. Given this, it is crucial that you keep working on yourself to ensure you stay ahead. The business of Me, Inc. or the business of managing you as a business has taken a lot more importance in these recessionary times.

When I passed out of college with my marketing degree, building a brand was reserved for material things you could buy. With globalisation and technology, all of us have also essentially become products with a set of features and benefits and companies are trying to buy the products which best fit their requirements.

The difference, though, compared to, say, fifteen years ago is that we as humans have become commoditised. Every person who applies for a job seems to have similar qualifications and experience. Similarly, most of your peers will have similar skill sets and abilities as you. As a result, it's become essential that you manage yourself almost like a business and learn and implement the skills of building a product (You), branding the product, marketing the product and selling the product.

This chapter is more than just about how to promote yourself, market your skills or building your reputation. It focuses on how you can go about building your image and influence people's perceptions in a manner which will help you rocket your career to new levels.

1. What's in a Name? Everything. Building Your Brand

I still remember how the brand Xerox became synonymous to photocopying to such an extent that irrespective of the photocopy machine used it used to be referenced as Xerox. There are plenty of examples like Coca Cola, FedEx, Google, Skype, etc. which have either defined the industry they were in or have become verbs. Now, that's the power of a brand.

Your personal brand is similar to any other corporate brand or product branding. It is the total experience of someone having a relationship with who you are and what you represent as an individual.

Branding yourself keeps you current in your chosen field, opens doors for you, and creates a lasting impression on clients. By developing your own brand, you'll have control over people's initial perception. If you don't brand yourself, someone else will, and the outcome might not be in your favour.

A brand goes through five levels of development.

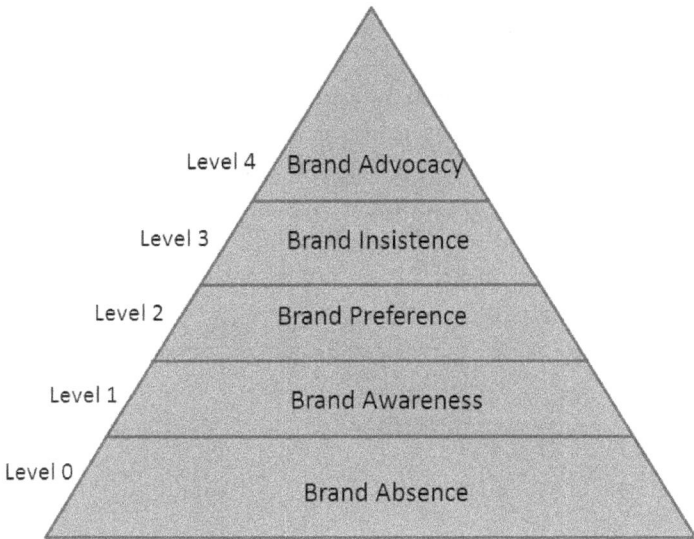

i.   Brand absence.

This is when you are new to an organisation, a business unit or a department. You arrive on the scene with little or no brand recall. In other words, you are a nobody!

ii.   Brand awareness

This is when people within your department and organisation start to know you. Your name sometimes comes up in discussions; you may be talked about during discussions of potential projects and other opportunities.

iii.   Brand preference

This is when you as a brand has established a presence and is known to a majority of the people. This is when people have a preference towards you. For example, your boss may choose to give you an opportunity compared to your colleague due to the trust and credibility you have built. A lot of people get to this stage and stop. While this level by itself can be rewarding, there's much more to achieve in the next two levels.

iv.   Brand insistence

This is often an exciting and scary level. When your brand is at this level, you are someone who is often fiercely sought after to lead projects, key initiatives, and strategic discussions. People want to have you on their projects due to the value you bring to the table. The level is scary because with insistence comes expectations to deliver. Once you have built your brand to this level, you will need to continuously work towards raising the bar higher.

v.   Brand advocacy

This is when you have people marketing you. Your name comes up first in meetings and discussions when there are topics discussed in your area of expertise. You are also recommended to be part of cross-departmental initiatives and are advocated to roles and responsibilities beyond your immediate line of duty.

Branding yourself is now a niche within the self-development industry and there have been some great books written on the subject. This book is not meant to be a compendium of branding ideas; rather it focuses on five top tips which I have used in building my personal brand

a) What's your USP?

The days of the generalist are over. When my father worked, they used to have General Managers, a concept introduced to denote a person responsible for the general functioning of a department, a business unit or organisation. While today you are still expected to have a general understanding of the various functions within the business; what's more important is your speciality.

Spend some time soul searching to find out what you are good at. Find and develop your unique selling proposition (USP). The term USP, which first became popular in the world of marketing, was the reason why consumers would buy your product instead of the competitor's. A personal USP is similar and is the reason why people will hire you or choose you over your colleagues.

A USP need not be a single thing; it could be a combination of skills coming together to provide a unique benefit. For example, one of the USP's that I developed initially was my ability to simplify technical jargon speak to business language. It still is my USP and my managers and customers love it when I can simplify the message.

b) Make your presence felt.

Once you have identified and developed your USP's, you need to promote them. A good product or service is of no use unless you market it to the right audience. Look out for opportunities where you can demonstrate your skills and demonstrate your strengths.

For example, if you like writing, look out for opportunities where you need to write a report or if you are good with presentations, volunteer to create presentations for your manager. One cool way to make a mark is to develop a personal catchphrase which can help people remember you. Luckily for me I found this in my name. I would introduce myself as "Hi. My name is Vipin Ramdas. That's V-I-P-I-N as in Very Important Person In Need."

Don't be afraid to speak up when you are in meetings, especially if there is something which you can contribute to. The whole point here is for people to know you and what you bring to the table.

c) **Create awareness.**

Like most marketers know, a successful brand has 4 P's going for them. Product, Price, Place and Promotion. You need to make sure your Product (YOU) are in the right places. In short, the right people need to know about you.

Look out for networking opportunities to meet up with influential people within the organisation. Don't shy away from talking to senior executives and managers and find out about what's going on in the company and their departments.

d) Dress one level up

Are you aware that when someone meets you for the first time, they form an opinion of you in less than one second? The fact that others form an opinion about you the moment they see you demonstrates how vitally important it is to dress for success.

Do not overlook the importance of dressing when it comes to your personal branding. While dressing up well will not guarantee you success, poor dressing will most likely rob you of many opportunities. Dressing well does not mean that you have to be moving around in a business suit. Depending on the culture of your organisation, choose an appropriate wardrobe.

Observe the movers and shakers in your company and make an attempt to dress well. Learn to dress one level up, but don't overdo it.

So, for example, if your colleagues wear T shirts while your manager moves around in formals, wear formals. On the other hand, if your manager is dressed casually, it's better to dress business casual rather than arrive in a business suit.

e) Manage your brand.

View your personal brand as a trademark: an asset that you must protect while continuously moulding and shaping it. Every time you are in a meeting, at a conference, networking reception or other event, you should be mindful of what others are experiencing about you and what you want others to experience about you. Those who know how to live and manage their personal brand will earn their respect in any situation.

2. Lose This, Lose Everything

Whether you're starting a new role or eyeing up a promotion, having a good reputation in the workplace is crucial for ensuring your continued success.

Having a good reputation will often result in being offered more interesting and challenging work and will ensure you are trusted to complete tasks autonomously.

The question to ask yourself is, "What will I stand for?" When people talk about you, what kind of words will they use? People with good reputations are often described with the following phrases: "a nice person," "easy to work with," "trustworthy," "honest," "optimistic" and "helpful." A bad reputation is often described as "abrasive," "pessimistic," "negative," "overbearing," "difficult," "unreliable," "selfish" or "deceptive."

A good reputation is not something that is achieved overnight; it's the product of persistent action over time. A good reputation is earned by saying the right things and following up with the right actions. Your reputation is formed by what you say, how you speak, and how you deal with others. Here are some of my tips on building a solid reputation:

a) Build trust

Trust is something which takes time to build but is very easily lost. One of the first things you need to do if you are to have a good reputation is to build

trust with the people you work with. Trust building happens in more than one way.

- Be honest. Don't be afraid to speak the
  truth.
- Be consistent. In words and behaviours. It's
  not enough to be trustworthy only on Tues-
  days and Thursdays.
- Maintain integrity: Walk the talk. Do what
  you say and say what you will do.
- Do the right thing.
- Use good judgement: Know what information can be shared, when to share it and
  with whom.

b) **Be reliable.**

Completing tasks when agreed (if not before), being
punctual and adhering to business processes and
protocols will enable colleagues and your superiors
to rely on you, making it much more likely that
they will trust you with new projects or greater responsibility.

c) **Show initiative**

If you think something can be done better, then let
your manager know so they are aware that you are
constantly evaluating your role and looking for improvements.

d) **Give and earn respect.**

No matter where you are in your organisation or
who you are talking to, learn to give respect to eve-

ryone you deal with. Whether this is the reception-ist, the cook in the canteen, your manager or a cus-tomer, everyone deserves to be treated with respect.

I consider this to be one of the most important skills everyone should possess. While not respect-ing your receptionist will not get in your way of your promotion, it could well hamper your person-al image and reputation in social gatherings.

e) Be tactful

Your opinion is valuable to the organization's growth and future. However, remember to offer it gently and with respect. For example, rather than inquiring why something is done a certain way, ask if management has ever considered doing it anoth-er way. Suggesting a new process rather than ques-tioning a current one highlights your forward thinking without insulting your boss's or the com-pany's approach.

f) Figure it out.

It's important to ask a lot of questions when you're new to any job, and your boss understands that. But don't pepper her with queries all day long.

You have to know when you need to go to your boss and when you don't. Try and seek help from other people within the company. Your supervisor will appreciate the fact that you've figured out how things work and that you've begun to build rela-tionships throughout the company.

70

The thing to understand about a reputation is that it sticks. As you start out in your career and begin building your reputation, people will label you with a good or bad reputation. If you have a good reputation, you can usually get away with doing some bad things while keeping your reputation intact. People may say things like "He strayed from the path," or "He had a lapse in judgment." Either way, they won't hold it against you for very long.

3. Blowing Your Horn without Going Deaf.

A lot of people have an aversion or fear of selling. If you offer them a task which involves selling anything, they will shy away from it. The fact is that all of us are selling ourselves at every stage of our life. We are trying to make a sale when we negotiate with our wife, kids, neighbours, storekeeper and anyone with whom you are trying to prove a point or convince. So selling is something which comes naturally to us. So why is it that when it comes to selling ourselves, we do such a poor job? It's because we have been told that it's not good to brag about ourselves because it's a sign of arrogance. It sure can sound like that if you don't know how to do it the right way.

When it comes to having a successful career, there is no substitute for hard (read "smart") work. But on the other hand, hard work won't do you any good if your accomplishments are going unnoticed.

You probably believe your work should speak for itself, and that the idea of tooting your own horn sounds, well, obnoxious. But waiting around hoping your good work will catch the boss's eye could be preventing you from getting the recognition—and possibly the promotions—you deserve at work. But how do you let people know about your good work without sounding like a brag pot?

Here are some tips I learnt which helped me toot my horn without feeling uncomfortable:

i.   **Keep track of your successes.**

This is something which I learnt slightly late in my career, but I have listed it here since it's the most important aspect in selling yourself. If you don't know what to brag about, how are you going to do it? Maintain a journal (physical or electronic) of all the accomplishments with as much details as you can. It's best to pen down all of these and you will be amazed at how much you actually achieve in your lifetime. It also gives you ready choices to include in your CV when you decide to look for another job!

ii. **Publicize your accomplishments.**

Seek out for opportunities to publicize your accomplishments. There are a number of ways you can do this. For example, you could publicize it to your boss in a weekly update report you send. You could also publicise it in project update reports, presentations or meetings. Do this discreetly by focussing on the accomplishment. Don't say, "I completed the research report on 25th Jan, two days ahead of schedule." Instead, put this more professionally by stating the due date and the completion date. People are smart enough to figure out that you delivered before time.

iii. Don't just tell them, show them.

If you want to be seen as genuine, you also need to let your work speak for itself. Show, don't tell. You've probably heard this saying since you were a kid, and it's a great reminder whenever you're tempted to tell someone how great you are. Instead of telling someone, find ways to show them instead—do your best work, kill it at that presentation, and graciously accept compliments for a job well done.

iv. Volunteer.

Look out for opportunities to showcase your expertise. Volunteer to take on work where you can demonstrate your abilities. There's nothing that works as good as your work. Apart from putting you in the limelight, it also demonstrates your willingness to go beyond your job description and brags about your flexibility and eagerness to be a team player.

v. Choose your audience.

Choosing your audience is crucial when it comes to bragging. There's no point only bragging away to your peers, as they will really not help you much in your career growth. Needless to say, you need to brag with your boss. Apart from this, find people who are the influencers and the movers and shakers within your organisation. Talk to them about your accomplishments during coffee breaks, before or after meetings, lunch breaks or anytime you have an opportunity to discuss it. Be careful not to force this down other people's ears. If you do, people may start avoiding you.

vi.   Choose your timing.

Once you get the right audience and the words in your mouth, you may wonder when you can use them. I've found is the best way to get started is not to wait for the big break (believe me, very few of us actually do get stuck in the elevator with the CEO). The best way is to take advantage of everyday situations where you can turn small talk into big talk.

vii.   Don't overdo it.

Lastly, make sure not to overdo this and come across as overconfident. Bragging is a skill and when done rightly will give you the right results and could backfire badly if overdone. Finding the right balance is definitely more art than science, but with a little practice and a lot of patience, you'll find having a healthy amount of confidence in your own abilities will soon grab the attention of those around you as well. No obnoxious boasting required!

Step 5: Taming the Lion: Every King Needs a Kingmaker

Show me a man who is a good loser and I'll show you a man

who is playing golf with his boss.

- Jim Murray

The phrase "lion taming" paints a picture of a dashing man in a top hat and tails, twirling a chair and cracking a whip at growling big cats. Indeed, that's what the lion taming acts of the circus have generally looked like, and they've been taking place for over 200 years. A lion is a wild animal with 3-inch (7.5-centimeter) claws and a mouth that opens wider than your head is long – 1 foot (30 centimetres). Its jaws can crush a bull's spine. Makes you wonder why anyone would even attempt to tame this beast. But they do. You wonder how it's done, and more importantly, why?

The why is what literally drives the "how." Man has this constant urge to be in control. To be in control of anything that can influence or impact his life. Especially if the object is someone or something perceived to be more powerful than the self, we derive an extreme sense of pleasure, joy and satisfaction in controlling this power.

Taming a lion simply means approaching something intimidating and powerful and using your wits and learned strategies to disarm the beast. In the corporate world, it's a very common metaphor used to describe how one can tame (read "train") one's manager or anyone in a position of power. People in power include your immediate manager, leaders within your organisation or a high profile customer.

If there's one relationship which is important in your life after your family and friends, it's the one with your boss. Think about it. An average person spends more than 90,000 hours at work in his lifetime. That's close to 25% of your life if we assume a work span of forty-four years. In a day, we most likely spend more time with our bosses than with our own partners. Scary, isn't it? So why is it that while we work hard at developing and nurturing every other relationship, we often do not give the same importance to our relationship with our bosses?

The first thing we need to understand is our bosses are just like us. They are people who have dreams, people with desires, people who want to be successful. We need to stop looking at our bosses like someone who came from outer space. So if managers are just like us and not aliens from Mars (or Venus), we should be treating them in the same manner as we expect others to treat us.

In this chapter I provide you some simple suggestions to help you build, nurture, leverage and benefit from your relationship with your boss. It will help you establish your own presence, authenticity, and credibility in the eyes of your boss and other leaders.

1. Seek First to Understand, Then to Be Understood

This is the 5th Habit in Stephen Covey's best-selling book *The 7 Habits of Highly Effective People*. Here he stresses the importance to use empathic listening to be genuinely influenced by a person, which compels them to reciprocate the listening and take an open mind to being influenced by you. This creates an atmosphere of caring, and positive problem solving. Here are my five top tips on how you can understand your manager better:

a) Understand his management style.

Every boss has their unique leadership style and management mantras. Make an effort to understand his communication style: is he direct, aggressive or submissive? Is he a helicopter manager or someone who believes in empowerment? What's his decision-making style (directive, participative, consultative, etc.)? The key here is to adapt to his style of management. You don't have to give up your identity and try and be someone else. All you need to do is understand his needs and meet them. Trust me: it's easier than it sounds.

b) Agree rules of engagement.

This one is very important. When you have a new manager, it's extremely important that you sit down with your manager and agree on how you will engage with him. Depending on the leadership and management style, managers will have different needs regarding how much information they want, how frequently, how decisions are made and how much involved they want to be in the day to day operations and management.

c) Discuss his goals and objectives.

One thing I have learned to do is to discuss my manager's goals and objectives. All of us usually will have goals defined for us based on the company's goals and the department or business unit's goals. However, as we now know, bosses are people too and they have dreams and aspirations too. Your manager will be glad that you discussed his needs and wants and will be even more grateful to know that you are there to support him.

d) Show and give respect.

"My boss is a jerk." This is probably what a lot of people think of their managers. A common complaint I hear from people is that their boss does not understand anything about work around there. Acknowledge that your boss is in the position because of things which he knows and does which you don't. He is not expected to know everything about what is going on. He has people like you to help him with things he does not know. Respect him for what he knows and what he does.

e) Define what success means to him.

Success has a different meaning to everyone. If you are to be seen as successful, you have to ensure that you achieve success as your boss would like to see it. What this simply means is to have a clear understanding of how your boss looks at successful tasks, projects, initiatives or anything else related to the job. So the next time you are assigned a task, initiative or a goal, be very specific and ask questions about your manager's expectations and define the critical success factors for them.

2. Manage Your Manager

This is probably one of the most talked about topics when it comes to your relationship with your boss. Once again, there are plenty of books, articles and blogs sharing some great information.

a) Learn to manage expectations.

Once you have understood your manager's working style, his communication style and his goals and objectives, you have defined what is effectively your playground or the boundaries within which you have to operate. The next part is playing by the rules of the game. This starts with managing your manager's expectations. This is really an on-going activity which you have to keep working at so that what you deliver is in line with your manager's expectations.

This requires you to have open lines of communication, healthy disagreements, openness to criticism and new ideas and the ability to get out of your comfort zone. Push back and set realistic deadlines if you think your manager is being unrealistic about his expectations. Don't shy away from asking for more time, and more importantly, don't be afraid of asking for help. A lot of people shy away from saying "I don't know." It's okay that you don't know how to do something; you are not expected to know everything. What is expected is that you ask the questions and seek out timely help instead of trying to do it all alone. Remember that your manager's job is to keep pushing you to make sure you deliver results, so it's essential that you proactively manage the expectations so as not to set yourself up for failure.

Here are my five simple tips for managing expectations:

1. If appropriate, get written agreement on what the end result will look like along with the timelines.
2. Have a clear understanding of the critical success factors.
3. Ensure you have the access to the right resources and help if required.
4. Maintain regular communication.
5. Once a task is complete, follow up to see how you did against the expectations.

b) Keep him informed

We are in the information era and communication is essential to the success of any business today. With more and more people working from remote offices, different geographical locations and from home, communication has taken on an even more important role in our work today.

Fortunately, technology has come to our aid and communication today is far easier than what it was fifteen years ago. Email, telephone, video conference, chat, etc. make communication easier, faster and cheaper. Once you have an understanding of your manager's communication needs, stick to them. That's it. If he does not define any specific communication guidelines, use the below as the basic rules:

1. Send a weekly summary report (email should do) of what you achieved during the week.
2. Keep him informed about progress of critical tasks, initiatives or projects. No manager likes surprises.
3. Always let him know of any hurdles or setbacks you face and make sure you tell him how you dealt with them. This demonstrates your thinking and problem-solving abilities.
4. Make sure you make your work known to him. Be subtle with this ensuring that you only focus on significant achievements. Don't overdo this.
5. Don't rely too much on email. Talk to your manager often using telephone, face to face or via video conference as convenient.

c) **Always be thinking strategically. Big picture.**

One big mistake a lot of young professionals make is to fail to see the big picture. You've probably heard this before and wondered "What is the big picture?"

Seeing the big picture requires you to see beyond yourself, your department or business unit and see things in the wider perspective, very often in the context of the corporate goal. As an example, if you are a part of customer service who attends to calls from customers, it is important to understand that you are not just there to address queries from customers. You are playing a much bigger role for your organisation. Your interaction with the customer and the experience you give him will influence the customers view and perception about your organisation. As you move up the corporate ladder, this is one quality which will separate you from the herd.

d) Answer questions your boss didn't ask. Anticipate.

Give more than you think you should. Learn to think beyond the obvious and make an effort to anticipate possible questions or clarifications your boss needs.

You are not a computer who simply follows instructions and produces a defined output. You are blessed with a creative intellect. Use it to feed your boss with information which you think will be useful and aids his decision making process.

For example, if you are asked to provide some statistics, look for opportunities to observe trends and mention them in your email or report. Similarly, think through the questions someone may have when they look at your email or report and include answers to them in your communication. If appropriate, you can also cheat and show the email or report to your colleague and ask if he has any questions.

e) Solicit feedback.

You need to know how you are doing. Ask for feedback from your manager from time to time about how you are doing in meeting his expectations. Look for subtle hints in your day to day interactions with your manager. If your boss displays a constant behaviour or requests something frequently, discuss with him if he would like you to formalise it. For example, if he keeps coming back to you asking about the status of a particular project, construct a formal update and send it to him in advance at an agreed frequency.

f) Help him succeed

While a lot is discussed and written about how you need to be successful, not the same amount of information is available on how can people help their bosses be more successful. After all, when your boss succeeds, not only does he or she gain a better reputation, so do you, and it also usually means your team is doing better work.

g) Get things done. Results matter.

Once you have understood your boss's priorities, objectives and goals, work with him to draft a plan on how you can support in achieving those goals. Once the plans are agreed, get on with it and focus on getting things done. At the end of the day, if you are not delivering results, none of the other things matter. Remember that you are working for a business which is operating to make profits, and profits come from delivering results. Here are my top tips on how to make sure you are seen as a finisher:

1. Always stick to deadlines unless your boss agrees to move the deadline.
2. Deliver more than what was expected.
3. Take things to a completion and don't leave them halfway, no matter how trivial the task may seem.

4. Focus on quality. Make sure your deliverables are the best in terms of content and presentation.
5. Be low maintenance. While you should ask your boss for help when you need it, make sure you have exhausted your options before you approach him. Your boss's time is valuable and no one likes to hand hold you for every task.

h) Be a problem solver.

Your boss has enough problems of his own. Don't go to him with more unless you also have answers to the problems. This does not mean you should not inform your manager about issues or challenges. It simply means that when informing your boss about your problem; also provide alternative solutions and your recommendation with reasons.

i) Build credibility and trust.

Your boss needs to be able to trust you to do a job as good as he would do it. This is your end goal with every task you do and every interaction you have with him. Once you get to this stage life becomes very easy and you will be able to influence a lot of your manager's decisions. Credibility and trust take time to build and they are something which you have to infuse into every step of your career.

j) Volunteer to offer help. Go the extra mile.

During the first four years of my career when I was not yet a manager, I used to wonder what managers did at their desks. They were busy preparing reports, conducting meetings, attending training and meeting senior managers.

I used to think how cool a manager's life was. It's only after I became a manager did I realise how different life is once you have to manage people. Your manager has a lot of things to attend to apart from the day to day operational stuff. Managers are often torn between Senior Management and their team members. During such times, if you volunteer to offer help or support them in taking on any tasks for them, it will go a long way in building your relationship. This attitude shows proactivity and a sensitive attitude and respect for your managers time. As you progress in your career you will learn to appreciate your manager and his work. When you move into a manager's shoe, you may be faced with the challenge of managing people who are older than you. Download a bonus chapter on "The Gen Y Manager: Tips on managing Gen X and Baby Boomers" by visiting http://myworkmywaybook.com.

Investing time and energy in building a professionally rewarding relationship with your manager will go a long way in your career progression. Your end goal should be to build trust and confidence with your manager so that he becomes an advocate and brand ambassador for you. Happy taming!

Step 6: Sharpen Your Corporate Axe: Even the Best Product Needs Upgrades

You are either moving forward or backwards. The fastest way to move backwards is to stand still.

There's a very famous story about sharpening the saw which is what inspired the title of this chapter. There is this man who stumbles upon a lumberjack in the mountains. The man stops to observe the lumberjack, watching him feverishly sawing at a very large tree. He notices that the lumberjack is working up a sweat, sawing and sawing, yet going nowhere.

The bystander notices that the saw the lumberjack is using is about as sharp as a butter knife. So, he says to the lumberjack, "Excuse me, Mr. Lumberjack, but I couldn't help noticing how hard you are working on that tree, but going nowhere." The lumberjack replies with sweat dripping off of his brow, "Yes...

I know. This tree seems to be giving me some trouble." The bystander says, "But, Mr. Lumberjack, your saw is so dull that it couldn't possibly cut through anything." "I know", says the lumberjack, "but I am too busy sawing to take time to sharpen my saw."

In this story, it is pretty obvious that if the man took a few minutes to sharpen his saw, he would be able to save a lot of time afterwards. However, in real life, it isn't always so obvious when we need to stop and "sharpen the saw."

If you've read *The 7 Habits of Highly Effective People* by Stephen Covey, you'll know that the seventh habit is called "Sharpen the Saw." (If you have not read this book, I highly recommend it – the writing is light and easy to follow, and the information is good.) Sharpening the saw means taking the time to recharge your batteries, improve on your skills, and generally taking care of yourself so you can be the best professional you can be.

Sharpening the saw doesn't mean just being thoughtful about the work you do – it means taking the time to take care of yourself – and your own productive capacity – so that you can have sustainable, productive success. From skills development and training to family time and vacation, sharpening the saw can have a different focus for everyone, but the core meaning is the same: you must respect yourself in order to make the most of your abilities. So what does it mean to sharpen the saw in a corporate career? I sum it up in three words: grow, nurture and act.

1.   The Tao of Growth.

The Japanese are known for their quality of work. One of the quality management techniques I particularly like is Kaizen.

Kaizen means "improvement" – "kai" means change/make better, and "zen" means good – but as the term is used as a business process it more closely resembles in English "continuous improvement." Kaizen is one of the keys to the steady improvement and innovation found at successful companies in Japan such as Toyota.

The overriding principle of Kaizen is that it is daily, continuous, steady, and it takes the long-term view. Kaizen also requires a commitment and a strong willingness to change. The interesting thing about Kaizen is that big, sudden improvements are not necessary. Instead, what is important is that you're always looking for ideas – including even the smallest of things – which you can build on. Keep moving forward. Here are some of my tips on how to implement the principles of Kaizen in your corporate life:

a)   **Identify your professional goals.**

Take time at the beginning of each year to think through what you would like to achieve during the year professionally. This could include a variety of things like gaining a better understanding of your industry, making new contacts, gaining an understanding of processes, etc. The idea is to have goals which you can measure at the end of the year.

b)   **Break down goals into bite-sized objectives.**

Once you have defined your goals for the year, break these down into bite-sized, achievable milestones. One of the principles of Kaizen is to keep making small changes which slowly add up to a larger goal. Say, for example, you want to learn about a new technology in your industry. You are obviously not going to be able to master it immediately. In this case you could break it down to objectives for each quarter so that you can see the progress you are making.

c)   Bring small changes.

This is probably one of the most important principles of Kaizen. The trick here is to make a commitment to improve yourself on a daily basis. These could be very small changes. It could be as simple as making sure you say "Good Morning" to your colleagues or spending some time with your colleagues every week outside the office. Don't let a single day pass by without making small improvements in your life. Read books and newsletters, look up news about your industry, anything which will add value to you as a professional.

d)   Get out of your comfort zone.

Growth happens only when you get out of your comfort zone. Your comfort zone is where you are at peace doing what you know and have probably mastered. If you are to grow, you need to be bold and venture out into areas which you have never explored. Don't be afraid to take on tasks or projects where you have no prior experience or skills. You will learn them on the job, which, in my opinion, is the best way to learn. If you have stage fright and fear giving a presentation, enrol for a course and present to smaller audience first. That audience could even be your spouse or children or your closest friend with whom you are comfortable. The idea is to DO IT so that you face your fears head on.

e)   Do a half-yearly assessment

You can't improve what you don't measure. Perform a half yearly assessment of how you are doing and what you have achieved during the past six months. During the course of the year, maintain a logbook of what you learn each day and how you have improved. Reflect on things which you could not achieve (yes, this will happen), and identify how and what you could do differently to make sure you achieve the goal going forward.

2. The Professional. Mastering the Skills.

The word "profession" is defined by Dictionary.com as "following an occupation for a livelihood or gain." From that definition, we are all in some form of profession. A professional is someone who conforms to the standards of that profession. Every profession has its own sets of standards, however, there are a few overarching principles which apply to all professions

a) Develop core values

i.   Integrity

You've heard this before a number of times and I can't emphasize the importance of this enough. You must walk the talk and talk the walk. Be trustworthy in all that you do – never deliberately mislead, whether by withholding or distorting information.

ii.   Honesty

Be honest no matter what the situation. Have the courage to speak the truth no matter what the consequences. A lie may get you out of the situation, but it will come back to bite you some day.

iii.   Empathy/Compassion

Have empathy and compassion for people. Always remember that you are dealing with people who have emotions and feelings. Learn to see other people's point of view in a conversation and be genuinely interested in understanding their arguments. You don't have to agree but you should make an effort to understand. A true professional is willing to help his or her co-workers when they are overburdened. He or she isn't afraid to share knowledge, opinion or simply an extra pair of hands.

iv.   Accountability

Take full responsibility for your actions and don't blame others if things go wrong. Do your job to the best of your capabilities. Ask yourself this simple question when performing any task: "If I owned this company, would I do a better job?"

v.   Respect

Show respect for your colleagues, peers, boss, receptionist and everyone else in your organization. Treat people the way you would expect people to treat you. Do not discriminate based on age, sex, country, colour, designation or anything else.

vi. Courage

Have and show the courage to do the right thing. Stand up for something which you believe is right and don't be afraid to voice your view.

vii. Work Ethics

Have strong ethics in the workplace. You don't have to be serious at work, but be sincere. Respect the work timings laid down by the company. Do not misuse company resources. Perform your job to the same standards as you would if you owned the company.

b) **Work on your people skills**

If there is one thing you need to master, it's the art of working with people. In Chapter 2, I discussed at length the importance of having good inter-personal skills. As you move up the corporate ladder there are some other skills which you need to develop.

i. **Accept and manage conflict.**

It is inevitable that you will occasionally have disagreements with your co-workers, or even your boss. Don't let yourself lose control. No matter how upset you are or how strongly you believe you are right, screaming isn't allowed, nor is name calling or door slamming. And it should go without saying that physical attacks should always be avoided, no matter what. Accept that you will have conflict at work and apply these five simple steps to manage conflict:

1. Stay Calm.

There are some memorable lines from the famous Rudyard Kipling poem "If":

If you can keep your head when all about you are losing theirs and blaming it on you. If you can trust yourself when all men doubt you. But make allowance for their doubting too...

After several verses the poem concludes: "Yours is the Earth and everything that's in it. And – which is more – you'll be a man, my son."

Even when provoked, keep a close hold on your temper; stay as calm as you possibly can.

2. Seek first to understand and then to be understood.

Each person has a unique point of view and people rarely agree on every detail. Being right is not what is important. When managing conflict, seeking the "truth" can trap you rather than set you free. For example, consider the differing testimony of witnesses that all see the same car accident. Truth is relative to the person's point of view. Keep emotions at bay and discuss what each other's objectives are and try and find a shared goal or shared purpose. This will help in the discovering potential solutions.

3. Acknowledge there is a problem.

Acknowledging the presence of a problem is the first step towards resolving it. Accept that there could be improvements on both sides and work towards a shared purpose/goal.

4. Brainstorm to find a solution.

Resolving conflicts is a creative act. There are many solutions to a single problem. Generate several possible solutions to the problem by collectively brainstorming ideas. Write down the various ideas generated and work through the list to reach a mutually acceptable solution.

5. Seek a mediator.

If you can't find a solution, agree to disagree and get a mediator who can help you reach a consensus.

ii. Be a team player.

Part of being successful at work is having the skills to work together with your co-workers and be a valuable part of the team. Being a good team player isn't always easy. Teams are usually created to solve difficult problems, and they often have tight deadlines and strict budgets. But this can be your chance to shine. Look at teamwork as not only a challenge, but as a great opportunity. Support other people on your team by offering positive feedback and providing help if they need it. Your willingness to collaborate and help others will make a good impression on both the group and upper management. Share information and resources with your team. Remember, you're all there for one purpose – and by keeping everyone informed, you contribute to that goal. If you have past experiences or knowledge that can help others, then offer it. They'll appreciate the help.

iii.   Work on communication skills.

Communication, when done well, sets you apart from other young professionals. Good communication is a strong asset, so learn it while you're in the beginning stages of your career. Keep working on the communication skills I talked about in Chapter 2.

c)   Develop Leadership Qualities

*   **Take ownership.**

Taking ownership means taking charge, or responsibility, of your work task to see it through from start to finish. This essentially means to act as if you are an owner of the business, whether you actually are or not. While on the face of it this sounds like a good advice, it's not as easy to follow. The simple reason being in most cases you do not own the business. So how then do we develop the sense of ownership? The way to do this is to separate yourself from the organization and bring personal credibility and reputation at stake. In other words, if you had to rate the work you did, what would be your score? This will push you to deliver beyond your expectations. From my personal experience, I can tell you that this is one quality which will earn you a lot of respect no matter what level you are or what kind of work you do.

- **Quit Whining.**

This one's straight and simple. Every company you work for, whether it's Google or IBM or Microsoft or General Motors, will have issues and will mess up from time to time. The fact is that if they didn't mess up, many other companies would be out of businesses. Similarly, if everything were perfect, then companies would not need people or tools to improve them. So stop whining about the problems you have at work. Do something to change the circumstances. If you can't, then accept it and move on and get on with your work.

- **See the Big Picture.**

Businesses exist to make a profit, but they also exist to make a difference or to provide a service or product that meets a need. Through work, individuals can make a difference and be part of a meaningful legacy. One thing you will need to learn is to see the big picture. You will hear this often from your management. What this essentially means is that you need to put your work and the tasks you undertake in perspective of the larger goals. In other words, you need to be able to think beyond your task as a mere activity. There will be times when you will be required to bite the bullet and go along with your colleagues even if you don't agree with their point of view. This will be to support the larger picture or the broader view of the organization.

When you understand how you daily activities align with the organization's purpose, values and goals, then work becomes more meaningful. And when you see the organization from this broad perspective, you focus on results that make a difference.

- **Be proactive.**

This is a quality which differentiates great leaders from the good ones. Leaders are never satisfied with the status quo and like to challenge things. They cannot sit in one place waiting for things to happen or be given orders. Leaders are proactive and take charge of situations. They are quick to spot opportunities and take decisive action to yield results.

- **Find a mentor.**

All great leaders have a mentor to support them. A mentor is someone whom a leader can confide it and can talk to about his issues and concerns and bounce ideas off of. A mentor is someone who has experience in the field and can share his knowledge. If you would like a mentor but can't find the right one at work or prefer to have one outside of work, visit http://www.myworkmywaybook.com and register to get a discount for one on one coaching from me.

3. Act One Step Ahead

You have to first believe what you want to BE and BE what you want to BE so that you BE what you want to BE. If you want that promotion, you need to act like you are already in that position before you get it. Very rarely will someone get a position for which he has not demonstrated skills and capabilities. In other words, learn to look out opportunity before security, responsibility before authority, and accountability before recognition.

If you want to become a leader, don't wait for the fancy title or the corner office. You can begin to act, think, and communicate like a leader long before that promotion. Even if you're still several levels down and someone else is calling all the shots, there are numerous ways to demonstrate your potential and carve your path to the role you want.

Always walk and act one level above your current role. Study the people who are in these positions and observe their behaviour. Find out what it is that they do differently, how they dress, how they talk, who they hang out with, and what kind of words they use. Study their behaviour whenever you get an opportunity.

Here are some tips on how you can stay above the pack. These activities send the signal that you aspire to leadership potential:

a) **Have a "Let me take that on "attitude.**

Offer to take on work which your boss has to complete. This will help you learn the kind of stuff your boss does apart from making a good impression with your manager. Make sure this "let me take that on" attitude extends beyond your relationship with your boss. Raise your hand for new initiatives, especially ones that might be visible to those outside your unit. This will give others a taste of what you'll be like in a more senior role.

b) Look out for those grey areas.

These are always problems that others aren't willing to tackle or don't even know exist. Every organization has needs that nobody is paying attention to, or people are actively ignoring. For example, there might be a process which is costing the company money but people are too busy to look at it. Or there is a particular business case which needs to be drafted to justify an investment. When you take on a task that no one else is willing to do, you make yourself stand out.

c) Help your boss succeed.

I've talked about this at length in Chapter 5 and want to stress the importance here again. You have to execute on your boss's priorities. Show her that you're willing to pick up the baton on important projects and lead them. Look to ways of how you can say yes rather than no whenever your boss asks you to help with something new. Find out what keeps your manager up at night and propose solutions to those problems.

d) Take on any leadership opportunities you get.

Keep a watch out for any opportunities you get to lead a team or group of people. It doesn't matter what kind of opportunity it is as long as you are asked to coordinate a set of people and tasks. This could also be social opportunities like organising events or being a lead on a particular project or initiative.

Taking the time to hone and refine your skills makes you much more productive and efficient. Because you are better at doing things, it actually takes you less time to do them, and you do them better. Even accounting for the time you spent on improving your skills, you still get your stuff done quicker. As an example, just learning to use a computer can save you ten or twenty hours of productive time every week for the rest of your career. I take time every single day to sharpen my saw. If you want to do more have more, and become more – you must do the same. So decide to start right now and make a list of things you need to improve on. Sharpen your saw!

Step 7: Dispel the Biggest Career Myths. The Moment of Truth

Reality is merely an illusion, albeit a very persistent one.

- Albert Einstein

Myths are a part of our lives. Webster's defines myth as "an idea or story that is believed by many people but that is not true." All of us have different sets of beliefs and opinions about a number of things and all of us like to believe that what we feel and know is the absolute truth. The myths that affect us most, in theory and usually in fact, are those that blend empirical truth with fiction.

The more truth they contain, the more convincing they are, the harder they are to refute, and therefore the more influence they have. The people who tell a myth do not judge it by whether it can be proven factually true, either. Rather, the myth is a sort of lens through which they see the world.

The fact of the matter is that while for one person something may seem like a myth, to another it is a not based on their own unique experiences. In this chapter I want to put across some of the ideas which were the beliefs I held in the initial years of my career and over the years have become nothing but myths.

Myth 1: I should become indispensable.

Truth: You will be forgotten before you walk out that door.

This is the biggest myth of them all. The belief that you need to be indispensable can seriously harm your career growth. Think about it. If you were indispensable, then that means no one else could do your job. This in turn means that the company would never promote you or give you new opportunities because there would be no one else to do your job. So irrespective of where you are in your company currently or the level of skills you have in a particular area, always remember that you SHOULD be replaceable.

The scarier part is that it's very likely that the job which you do today will be replaced by a computer rather than another human being. Fifty years ago, factory jobs were a staple of life, and they employed nearly one-third of the workforce.

Factories produced all types of products for the consumer, from packaged foods to refrigerators or materials to build houses. A lot of these jobs have now been replaced by computerized machines that boost production and reduce the amount of labour required to make the products. Make sure you are continually working on enhancing your skills and self-development before they replace you with an app for the iPad or Android!

Myth 2: If I work hard I will get that promotion.

Truth: If you want it, you have to ASK.

There's nothing more dangerous than assuming that you
"deserve" something. Now, I don't mean to hurt anyone's self-
esteem or self-confidence. The point I want to get across is
you will get a promotion if your manager and anyone else
influencing or contributing to the decision believes that you
deserve the promotion.

In other words, you may believe that you are fit for the job
and have the required qualifications, skills and experience.
However, if the people who are making the decision don't
share this belief, you will not go too far. If you do, it won't be
fast enough. So how do you make sure you are considered
whenever there is an opportunity for a promotion? Simple.
Refer back to this book and read through Chapters 4, 5 and 6.

There has been a widely held belief for decades that those
hardest workers get the promotion. This is not true. The most
likable people get promoted. Your mother was right: Good
social skills are crucial to your career. Across the board, people
would rather work with someone who is likable and incompe-
tent than with someone who is skilled and obnoxious. Finally,
like one of my favourite motivational speakers Jim Rohn said,
"If you want something in your life, ASK."

Myth 3: The Company does not pay me enough.

Truth: Your employer pays you just enough so that you don't
quit and you work just enough so the employer does not fire
you.

This is one of the most common myths irrespective of which industry you are in and the kind of role you are doing. The funny part is that when you become a manager, you start believing that people are paid fairly for the same role that you did a few years ago. You accepted what your employer offered to pay you, so get on with your job and do a good job. Before you ask your employer for a pay rise, make sure you have done your research and have the facts with you. If it still does not work out, quit and move on, but stop whining.

Myth 4: It's business, not personal.

Truth: Everything is personal.

Let's face it. A business is people dealing with other people. So you cannot take the person out of business. People have feelings, and most people react to external stimuli. Can you imagine that Steve Jobs accepted it was "just business" when he was ousted from his position at Apple, the company that had been his brainchild? Can you imagine saying, "It's business, nothing personal" to any of the leaders, entrepreneurs, teachers, bosses, and CEOs who have spent half of their lives at work and put their heart and soul – and who knows how many years of their lives – into their work?

Business is very personal, because we each crave a deeper connection with our work, a connection that at one point in time transcends position and power and money, a connection in which we meet needs and create something. We all want to be valued and recognized. And we like to know that we are making a difference when we put our heart and soul into something. All of these give us a connection to our deeper self, the person within.

Myth 5: My work will speak for itself.

Truth: Even McDonald's needs to sell itself.

First things first. You need to be good at your job. However, that's often not enough. A good product is just the foundation (and a very important one) in ensuring you stay ahead at work. Every marketing manager knows the 4 P's of marketing: Product, Price, Place and Positioning. You and your work are your products. You still need to make sure you are marketing it to the right audience (place) and how you market yourself and your work (positioning) so that people perceive the right value (price) you provide.

Myth 6: I can job hop my way up the corporate ladder.

Truth: You will probably end up with a higher salary but not a higher position.

Job hopping means rapidly switching from one job to another; each job might last a year or less. I do think that with the options available these days, it's ok to job hop in the first four to five years of your career.

Job hopping does not always mean switching employers. It could be a different job in a different department. The reason I say this is that a lot of us (especially Gen Xers) took on default careers not always as a matter of choice, but based on the trend. I took up a job in sales as I majored in marketing, but then moved on to do a number of other things, including writing proposals, pre-sales, business analysis and then customer service.

While there could be few who have a clear idea of what they want to do, most of us need to go through a bit of trial and error to figure out what we want to do. One thing to remember though is that job hopping should be more to gain experience in different areas rather than as a tactic to move up the corporate ladder.

Myth 7: You have to be serious about your work.

Truth: You don't have to take your work seriously, but do it sincerely.

There's a difference in being serious about your job and being sincere. You workplace does not have to be a place where you are straight faced and you feel restrained to express yourself freely. Learn to loosen up and be humorous and crack a few jokes once in a while. The mind is the most creative when it is relaxed and at ease.

Your career can be joyous, sad, hard, easy, anxious, smooth, fast, slow, depressing, invigorating, and much more. A sincere person gives him or herself to the flow of life, accepting its swings, without being taken over by the temporary shifts.

Sincerity comes by doing things when no one's watching, by doing things because you know it's the right thing to do, not because you get paid to do it. When you are sincere about your work, it shows and it pays off in the long term.

Myth 8: My Company is responsible to provide me a career.

Truth: No one cares about your career if you don't.

If you are one of those who believes in this, now is the time to wake up. Your employer is paying you for your services. Period. They are not responsible to shape your career. There is only one person responsible for your career. YOU! So accept this truth and start taking charge of your career. If your employer is not providing you the opportunities to grow, then seek those opportunities elsewhere. I'm surprised at how many people expect their organisations to provide them a career path.

I firmly believe that with the number of opportunities these days you can choose your career path. You may have to accept a few pauses in the process, but by and large you have the ability to decide what you want to be doing. But first you need to know where you want to go and what it takes to get there. Once you have figured this out, go all out to develop yourself and you will soon see that opportunities soon start coming your way.

Myth 9: That's not my responsibility.

Truth: If you know about it, there's probably something for you in it.

All through my life I have been someone who has welcomed things my managers have asked of me. I have always approached things with an attitude to "do it" rather than finding a reason not to do it. This has sometimes got me into trouble and stressed me out, but in the longer term it has helped me to grow overall and learn some skills which I would never have dreamt of learning. For example, I took on myself a project of building a multimedia demo system for our company's software. I had no idea how I was going to do this as I had never done it before, but I was keen to learn it. I spent almost two years to finish the project but I can now probably write a book about producing a multimedia presentation. Now that I think about it, I will write a blog article on this if not a book.

The bottom line is that if something comes your way; make a very careful assessment if it is something which will help you grow in your pursuit of your goal. If it will, then take it on even if it means you have to work a few hours extra for a month or more. You will be surprised how the skills you learn will prove useful at some time in your career and you will be glad that you took on the challenge.

Myth 10: I can't stand this place. It's politics everywhere.

Truth: So long as you have people working in an organisation, you will see office politics. So bite the bullet and work through it.

Wikipedia has an interesting way of defining politics in the workplace. It says workplace politics (office politics or organizational politics) is "the use of power within an organization for the pursuit of agendas and self-interest without regard to their effect on the organization's efforts to achieve its goals." My problem with this definition is that it puts the word politics in a very negative connotation. It sends a message that office politics is always bad and harmful.

Politics simply refers to the dynamics and struggles for power. Most human relationships involve some kind of back-and-forth play for power. We contend for control at home on a daily basis – what to watch on TV, what to eat for dinner, where to go on vacation and so on. Around the office, where people with conflicting goals have to get along and careers are at stake, politics thrives. According to most experts, no workplace is immune to struggles for power. If we wish to foster good working relationships, get things done or get ahead, experts argue that we should actively and consciously engage in office politics.

Office politics is a subject which deserves a book in itself, but the first thing is that you need to deal effectively with office politics and use it yourself in a positive way; you must first to accept the reality of it. Once you've done this, you then need to develop strategies to deal with the political behaviour that is going on around you.

Myth 11: I don't work for money.

Truth: If they didn't pay you, would you stop working?

Ask yourself again: If you won the lottery tomorrow, would you go back to your job the next day? Work is about money. Unless you are already a millionaire and have all the time in the world, working is a need rather than a want. So accept the fact that you work for money. It's true that you don't work ONLY for money. There are other things like satisfaction, fulfilment, enjoyment, excitement, etc. But till the time you are financially free, all of these would not matter unless you had the money. So stop kidding yourself and make sure you get what you believe you deserve.

Myth 12: I will work hard now. I can enjoy life later.

Truth: The fact is the company doesn't care about your work-life balance if you don't.

A lot is being talked recently about having the right work-life balance and how organisations need to be sensitive to the needs of their employees and provide them a work-life balance. My view is that organisations are in business for one single purpose.

That purpose is profits (non-profit organisations are an exception). So organisations want maximum output with minimum input. Now, I don't mean to say that organisations are not sensitive to the need of employees having a good work-life balance.

Work-life balance is commonly attributed to providing time for people to have "enough" time to have a life outside work. The problem is who defines how much is "enough" and who defines what "life" is. The answer to that question is YOU. The simple fact about time is that you will never *find* time for anything. If you want time you must *make* it. At the end of the day, it's your perception of what work-life balance means to you, but don't be afraid to draw the lines with your manager or anyone else. While you need to be flexible from time to time and stay back to finish off that project report, no one should be allowed to dictate how you manage your life.

A Final Word

Your career is a marathon. Not a sprint.

One day, a business owner decided he'd had enough. Enough of the unremitting workload, enough of the lack of response, enough of the crushing loneliness.

He went into the woods to have one last talk to God. "God," he said. "Can you give me one good reason why I shouldn't quit?" The answer took him by surprise. "Look around you," it said. "Do you see the fern and the bamboo?" "Yes," the man replied.

"When I planted the fern and the bamboo, I took very good care of them. I gave them both equal amounts of food and water. I gave them sunlight in spring and protected them from the storms in autumn. The fern quickly grew from the earth. Its brilliant fronds soon covered the forest floor.

"Yet nothing came from the bamboo seed. But I did not quit on the bamboo. In the second year, the fern grew even more splendidly than before, but nothing came from the bamboo seed. But I did not quit on the bamboo. In year three there was still nothing from the bamboo seed. But I would not quit. In year four, again, there was nothing from the bamboo seed. Still I would not quit.

"Then in the fifth year a tiny sprout emerged from the earth. Compared to the fern it was seemingly small and insignificant. But day by day, the sprout grew. First a shoot, then a seedling, and finally a cane. Within six months, the bamboo cane had risen to a height of 100 feet. It had spent the five years growing roots. Those roots made it strong and gave it what it needed to survive. I would not give any of my creations a challenge it could not handle.

"Did you know that all this time you have been struggling, you have been growing? Growing the roots that you need to produce your fruit. Your time will come. You will rise high."

"How high should I rise?" the man asked.

"How high will the bamboo rise?" asked God in return.

"As high as it can?" the man questioned.

"Yes," God replied. "Give me glory by rising as high as you can." The small business owner left the forest. And never went back.

The moral of the story: Don't assume that success is a race and that the winners are the first past the line. Don't think that, because you haven't succeeded in your goals yet, you never will. Don't conclude that, just because you can't see evidence of growth, you're not growing.

Believe in yourself, your dreams, and your goals.

Don't presume to know how things will turn out. Have joy in the journey and let the outcomes take care of themselves. As I come to the end of this book, I would like to leave you with some concluding thoughts.

1. Your career is a marathon, not a sprint.

Most of us are accustomed to instant gratification. We are used to watching movies "on demand" the moment we want to see them. We communicate in real time via text, IM, Twitter, and Facebook. We like getting something instantly, right when we want it. Today's technologies enable this, but they also create a damaging sense of impatience.

Take advantage of the early stages of your career to soak up as much knowledge as you can to build a sturdy foundation for a long and prosperous career. Be curious. Ask questions. Try to learn more about other areas of your business. This will help broaden your potential for more opportunities instead of pigeonholing yourself for the future.

You need to collect experiences throughout your career, whether that is with five employers or ten, with one business function or five, or in one country or three. The idea is that you need to be a lifelong learner if you want to make an impact, succeed and feel accomplished. The experiences you have expand your worldview, give you new perspectives and make you a more interesting person.

There is an age-old saying which goes "Good things come to those who wait." Many of the younger generation tend to ignore this and get disappointed way too early when their expectations are not met. Always make sure the opportunities you are pursuing have growth potential, but make sure that your expectations are in line, and that you are prepared to put in the necessary time to grow professionally. Ask yourself are you "going" through your career or are you "growing" through it.

2. Don't be afraid of failures.

You will fail your way to success. If you don't fail, how will you know what works and what doesn't? Thomas Edison once said, "I have not failed. I have found 10,000 ways that won't work."

While you may not get 10,000 opportunities to fail in a corporate environment, what's important to understand that failure is a part of learning. I know you have probably heard this before and probably think its foolish advice in the corporate world.

During the initial stages of your career, no one will expect you to take decisions or perform tasks which will become a matter of life and death for you or the company.

So relax and be bold enough to try new things, explore new opportunities, venture into unknown territory and get out of your comfort zone. Look for ways to say "yes" to requests from people without stressing yourself out. I assure you will not regret it.

3. Results matter.

Understand something and have it deep rooted into your being. Businesses exist to make profits, and profits come by producing results. So while you can do all the great things I have highlighted earlier and build relationships or work on personal development, unless you can clearly demonstrate value to your organisation, you will not go far. In fact, you may go out!

4. Recognize the two most important people in your career.

I can't stress the importance of this enough. There are only two people who matter the most in your career, YOU and your boss. During the later stages of your career, there will be more people who influence your career, but in the first few years, it crucial that you keep working on these two.

Focus your energy and time on self-development, building relationships, building your brand and establishing credibility and reputation. Learn how to work with your boss, and more importantly, make it your personal responsibility to help him succeed. Once your boss sees that you are here to help him succeed, it's a no brainer on who's getting that next promotion or big opportunity.

5. If you don't like it, shake it and move on.

Find a job you love, or love the job you have. If you can't do that, move on and find something you will love, but stop whining and complaining.

This is probably one of the most debated topics today. The choice between pursuing your passion and doing the safe thing that everyone else does.

To be honest, I don't think there is one right answer. It purely depends on your circumstances; phase in life, dreams and desires, and how strongly you feel about them. Each path has its ups and downs, pros and cons. The important thing is that no matter what you do, do it well.

The trouble I see these days is that everyone wants that exciting project, the next big opportunity and wants to do what excites them or ignites their passion. What's worse is that if they don't get it, they start blaming the company for not providing the right opportunities and challenges. The fact is that an organisation has specific goals and objectives and a limited number of resources with which to achieve them. So while there will be opportunities, they will be given to people whom the company believes will fulfil them the best. So your job is to make sure you work hard to make it difficult for the company to choose someone else for these opportunities which you are interested in. How do you do this? Since you have come this far in this book, I'm hoping you have the answer to that question.

My final word: If you don't like what you are doing, move on to something else. Believe in yourself, your skills and abilities and pursue your dreams. There is a great career out there for you, but no one but you can find it. I wish you all the success in your career. Define your work, don't let it define you.